PRAISE FOR *WHICH VOICE WILL YOU FOLLOW*

In an age when religion is attacked, maligned, and ignored, Bill Tuck presents an attractive approach toward faith that will interest the believer and unbeliever alike. This book presents a vibrant and thoughtful faith that is based in Scripture, grounded in theological insight, and always focused on ethical action. Pushing aside dogmatism and narrow provincialism, the book summonses the reader to a bold faith that invites questions, doubts, and misgivings as it seeks for meaning in an increasingly skeptical world. This book can rekindle the fires of devotion while challenging the reader to adopt a life of faith, love, and service.

Thomas Graves
President Emeritus, Baptist Theological Seminary at Richmond

This book is an excellent treatment of the question at the heart of all Christian belief and action, namely, how to think and behave as one who has "the mind of Christ" (Philippians 2:5). Tuck brings his years as pastor and professor to this insightful overview which blends biblical, theological and homiletical material. He speaks to the ecological crisis as well as the problem of personal moral development. Ministers seeking help for sermons, teachers developing materials for classes, or researchers needing solid guidance will find this a ready and reliable resource to which they will turn again and again.

Paul D. Simmons
Clinical Professor
University of Louisville School of Medicine & Dentistry

Dr. William Tuck (Bill) has a way of always illustrating his books with stories or quotations that are both apt and persuasive. Where many authors make statements and more statements, trying to argue their way from one chapter to another, Bill creates a kind of wave motion in which each assertion is followed not by another assertion but by a little gem of illustration, so that the reader is gently swept up and carried contentedly forward to the next point Bill wishes to make. The overall effect is subtle and pleasant, and we find ourselves reading more pages than we meant to at a single sitting and agreeing with what we have read as though it were a simplified and convincing version of Holy Writ.

This book, *Which Voice Will You Follow?*, is one of Bill's best. It speaks to the heart about who we are and how we can become better persons and better Christians than we have been, so that in the end we are happier and more delighted with life than we ever expected to be.

John Killinger
Former Professor at Vanderbilt Divinity School
Pastor and author of many books, including *The Tender Shepherd* and
Fundamentals of Preaching.

Dr. William Powell Tuck's ministry has shaped my own ever since I had him as a homiletics professor thirty-five years ago. His influence has endured because he has something to say — something grounded in Christian tradition, informed by scholarly thought, authenticated by personal experience, and enriched by creative illustrations. This influence (and all that shapes it) continues in Dr. Tuck's most recent book *Which Voice Will You Follow? Hearing and Answering Christ's Call.*

As the title indicates, this is a book about discerning the voice of Christ in the midst of many competing voices, but given the nature of this discernment and what is at stake in it, the book explores an array of critical tasks including the character of God, the nature of revelation, and the shape of Christian life. On each subject, Dr. Tuck provides helpful insights and practical wisdom without oversimplifying or trivializing matters. He is relevant without being trendy. He engages critical contemporary subjects like ecological concern and the question of suffering in a way that deepens thought without presuming to have all the answers. He balances the need for individual piety with the calling to pursue social justice.

Thus, again, Dr. Tuck has something to say, his influence continues. All with ears to hear are invited to listen – for the wisdom in this book and the voice of Christ.

Christopher Chapman
Senior Pastor, First Baptist Church, Raleigh, North Carolina

Other Books by William Powell Tuck

Facing Grief and Death

The Struggle for Meaning (editor)

Knowing God: Religious Knowledge in the Theology of John Baillie

Our Baptist Tradition

Ministry: An Ecumenical Challenge (editor)

Getting Past the Pain

A Glorious Vision

The Bible as Our Guide for Spiritual Growth (editor)

Authentic Evangelism

The Lord's Prayer Today

The Way for All Seasons

Through the Eyes of a Child

Christmas Is for the Young… Whatever Their Age

Love as a Way of Living

The Compelling Faces of Jesus

The Left Behind Fantasy

The Ten Commandments: Their Meaning Today

Facing Life's Ups and Downs

The Church in Today's World

The Church Under the Cross

Modern Shapers of Baptist Thought in America

The Journey to the Undiscovered Country: What's Beyond Death?

A Pastor Preaching: Toward a Theology of the Proclaimed Word

The Pulpit Ministry of the Pastors of River Road Church, Baptist
(editor)

The Last Words from the Cross

Lord, I Keep Getting a Busy Signal:
Reaching for a Better Spiritual Connection

Overcoming Sermon Block: The Preacher's Workshop

A Revolutionary Gospel:
Salvation in the Theology of Walter Rauschenbusch

Holidays, Holy Days and Special Days

A Positive Word for Christian Lamenting: Funeral Homilies

The Forgotten Beatitude: Worshipping through Stewardship

Star Thrower: A Pastor's Handbook

A Pastoral Prophet: Sermons and Prayers of Wayne E. Oates (editor)

The Abiding Presence: Communion Meditations

WHICH VOICE WILL YOU FOLLOW?

HEARING AND ANSWERING CHRIST'S CALL

WILLIAM POWELL TUCK

Energion Publications
Gonzalez, FL
2018

Adobe Digital Editions: 978-1-63199-527-9
Kindle: 978-1-63199-528-6
Google Play: 978-1-63199-529-3
iBooks: 978-1-63199-530-9

ISBN10: 1-63199-522-7
ISBN13: 978-1-63199-522-4
Library of Congress Control Number: 2018940043

Energion Publications
P. O. Box 841
Gonzalez, FL 32560

energion.com
pubs@energion.com

For

Bill, Angela, Campbell, and Alden

Special gifts of love along the Way

TABLE OF CONTENTS

PREFACE

G. K. Chesterton was a famous and outstanding English Christian writer of several decades ago. But he was noted to be one of the most absent-minded men to be so intelligent. He always seemed to have difficulty in keeping his dates straight and in remembering his schedule for lectures or class meetings. One time he sent a telegram to a friend and asked: "Am I coming to you tonight or what?" "Not this Tuesday but next Wednesday," his friend responded. The most noted of his state of confusion was the telegram he sent to his wife inquiring: "I am in Market Harborough. Where ought I to be?" "Home," she responded. She said later that it was easier to get him to come home and start from home than to tell him how to get where he ought to be from where he was.

Isn't it so for most of us? We know where we are this moment, but where ought we to be in life? We long for someone to tell us to come back home and then help us start off in the right direction. Many of us are no longer sure where home is any more. Voices from many quarters are screaming at us to follow their lead. We hear/see/feel them calling us to follow them down the paths of materialism, pleasure, financial security, sexual gratification, comfort, political loyalty, religious absolutism, bigotry, racism, modernism, and countless others. How do we discern the distinguishable voices from the illegitimate ones?

Even in the realm of religion many voices cry out to us to follow them. How do we determine the real voices from the false ones? There are so many religious voices from around the world with so many valuable insights and beliefs in all of them. Likewise, the Christian voices are mixed with fundamental certainty to agnostic Christianity, biblical literalism and inerrancy to prosperity gospel, the only true church to come as you are and leave as you came invitations, narrow-minded beliefs to anything goes philosophy, or an eternal quest for the truth with an openness to a growing faith. Many in our world today have turned a deaf ear to religion altogether and declare "none" as their faith perspective. They are weary with the summons to believe based on dogma, a religious book, church affiliation, the "final answers," or any narrow view of "spirituality." In the following pages, one believer seeks to show how he has tried to listen to the "voice" of Christ and follow him into an open and growing faith, striving to discern how to understand the "Christ-like" Way and to apply its high demands to his inner spiritual growth and to his daily living. I make no claim to having "the only answer" to a religious quest, but testify to what has given me meaning and direction in my own search for life's meaning. I have not found this approach always to be easy or simple, but it has given me assurance that I am following the true voice. I agree with Harvey Cox. "The time is ripe to retrieve the term 'Way' for Christianity and 'followers of the Way' for Christians."[1] I want to express my appreciation to my friend and fellow minister, Rand Forder, for proof-reading my original manuscript. He has helped me avoid some missteps along the way.

---

1   Cox, Harvey. *The Future of Faith* (New York: HarperCollins, 2009), 78.

CHAPTER 1

WHICH VOICE WILL YOU FOLLOW?

In one of the Peanuts cartoons, Linus tells Lucy that he has made an important theological discovery.

"Yeah," says Lucy. "What is it?"

"Well," says Linus, "I know why my prayers haven't been answered. I've been praying with my hands down, and you're supposed to hold them up like this!"

Oh, Linus, if it were only so simple, to be assured that when we have the proper prayer position, then we know we will be able to hear God's response to us. But so many voices demand our attention today. How do we discern the right one to follow, especially the divine voice?

THE OLD TESTAMENT STORY

An Old Testament story in 1 Samuel 3:1-10 reminds us of this dilemma. Many years ago, in a time much like our own, the word of God was rare and there were then like now no frequent visions of God. A young boy had gone to minister to an older priest named Eli whose eyesight was failing. That is probably the reason the boy slept close by him at night. He also stayed very close to the Ark of the Covenant, because one of his responsibilities was to keep the Eternal Flame burning near the Ark. The voice of God was rare in those days. Although many Sunday School quarterlies have depicted him as a young child, the boy was more likely from fifteen to seventeen years old. He was a teenager, we would say. In this story, Samuel was sleeping. He heard a voice in the night. As he had immediately done night after night, thinking that his master, Eli, was calling, he got up and went to see what needed tending to.

"I did not call," Eli says. He sends him back to his bed. But Samuel returns again, and again, and finally Eli realized that maybe it is the voice of God which is speaking to Samuel. He then instructs the young lad to say, "Speak, Lord, for your servant hears." The message of God is communicated to a young teenage boy about the judgment which God is sending upon this good man Eli and his family, because the sons of Eli were scoundrels and they had corrupted the house of God and His service. The message was not easily received and Samuel did not pass it on so quickly to Eli. But when Eli insisted he shared the message with him. God's judgment did come, and this young boy rose to be one of the great prophets in the land of Israel.

In the Old Testament, the voice of God came to several other people at numerous times. Abraham sensed the voice of God calling him to go to a land that he knew not where. Moses while he was on the back side of a mountain tending sheep, suddenly was confronted by a burning bush that was not consumed. And in that burning bush, he met the presence of God's spirit. Isaiah, went to the temple as was his custom, following the death of the great, beloved King of Israel, and he had a vision of God high and lifted up. Jeremiah, when he was a young lad tending his daily tasks, was confronted by the very presence and power of God as he called him into his service. Ezekiel, by the bank of a river in a strange land, was confronted by the power and presence of God. Paul, traveling to persecute the Christians in Damascus, had a great light overshadow him, and he sensed the very power and presence of God, and he too responded to the voice.

In the Scripture passage recorded in John 12:27-33, Jesus was struggling with the prospect of his death hanging upon the cross in the last hours of his life. We have a glimpse into his inner life and his personal dilemma as he cries out to know where God is amid his struggle and dying. He at first prays that he might be saved from this death, but quickly acknowledges that this is the reason he has come. He asks that God might be glorified, and a voice spoke to Christ. Some heard it; while others said that it only thunder. Some said that it was an angel speaking. It is interesting to recall that on some of the most significant times in the life of Christ, he heard the voice of God. He heard the voice of God at His baptism, on the Mount of Transfiguration, and in the moments reflecting on his dying. But the Jewish teachers taught in the day of Jesus that the voice of God was no longer heard. They believed that God's voice came only indirectly to persons. But the Scriptures tell us that Jesus heard God's voice directly on at least three occasions.

FOLLOWING CHRIST

When we turn to the New Testament, we find that Christians are called to follow Jesus Christ. In at least eight-seven references, the four Gospels denote Jesus saying to those who would become his disciples: "Follow me." His followers are called to be disciples or learners, called to be saints, called into fellowship with God's son, Jesus Christ, our Lord, called out of darkness, called to eternal life, called to liberty, and called according to His purpose. We are called to be possessed by Christ, who is Lord of all of life. As Christians, we probably would not debate today that the voice of God has come. But does the voice of God still come? Can you and I today still hear God addressing us in some way?

One of the reasons we sometimes have difficulty discerning what is the voice of God, is that there are so many voices demanding our attention and calling to us saying: "I am the way of life." Many voices call to us saying: "Walk within my way and you will have abundant living." "Take my way and you will share in plenty." "Take my way and you will feel delightful."

THE VOICE OF MATERIALISM

One of these voices today is the voice of materialism. This voice tells us that we are what we possess. What we have makes us who and what we are. It says that we in essence are judged by the things that we have. Too many of us too quickly and too foolishly fall into this kind of trap. Eugene Ionesco, in a short play entitled

The New Tenant, which was performed in Paris, tells about a man who was moving into his new apartment. The movers bring in a sofa, a table, a refrigerator, some chairs, kitchen furniture, and then they bring in two more sofas, and some more furniture. After a while the movers open the ceiling and begin to let furniture down through the ceiling. The room is completely filled up and piled high. Furniture has spilled over onto the sidewalk and into the River Seine. There is no more room and a voice asks: "Is there anything else we can do?" A voice from beneath the pile of furniture replies: "The light. Get the lights." "Right," the voice responds. And the light is turned off and the play comes to an end. What is the message? We are encumbered by our possessions. Our possessions possess us. Do not buy into the philosophy of life that tells you loudly and clearly that material things are the essence of what constitutes authentic living.

THE VOICE OF THE PLAYBOY VIEW OF LIFE

Another voice that we often succumb to is the voice that has sounded loudly and clearly for decades. And that voice is the playboy philosophy of life. This philosophy says that free sex is what really constitutes authentic living. This approach believes that one lives for instant gratification. This attitude has no high regard for another person. Persons are treated as things or as objects. Others are seen for the purpose of gratifying your sexuality. Others are there for your pleasure. No lasting commitments are made. Women are depicted as a plaything for men, a bunny. Sex is for the moment and no lasting relationships are established. They do not talk about marriage, because sex is merely for one's own gratification. This philosophy is sold to us through music, television, movies, the internet, books, and magazines. Many in our society have swallowed it hook, line, and sinker. Do not buy into that philosophy, because it is a dead-end street that will haunt us again and again with guilt and tragedy. The movies do not usually depict the outcome, the discards and the rejections that come from that kind of life. The

Church needs to challenge that philosophy clearly for the shallow approach to life that it is.

THE VOICE OF CHEAP AND CIVIL RELIGION

Also, do not listen to the voice that is calling us to cheap religion and civil religion. There are many voices in our land today which are telling us that religion is primarily something that focuses on rigid dogmatism, denominational loyalty, or confined to a way to make us feel good. If we have the right theological answers or belong to the "right" church, than we are authentic believers. Religion, for others, is a spectator's sport. If we are entertained, then we feel religious. When we get goosebumps, this approach affirms that this makes me right with God. An even more distorted view is the one that equates whatever my country wants with what is the essence of religion. And so we wrap God and country in the same flag and bow down and worship both country and God at the same shrine, and we never see that this is idolatry. Many who advocate this kind of philosophy of life call themselves very moral, yet they do not recall the judgment that came from the Old Testament prophets who thundered the warning that God is above country. We can never equate what one country does, no matter how good it is, as God's way. We cannot equate God and country, religion and the flag. Do not buy into cheap religion that offers us easy answers to complicated issues, salvation without commitment, grace without surrender, and redemption without sacrifice. Jesus calls us to take up our cross and follow Him.

THE VOICE OF SELFISHNESS

Do not follow that voice which rings within our ears telling us that the basic philosophy of life is "me-ism." Selfishness is the main concern of this approach. Whatever I want is the only judgment upon anybody else's importance. Every other person in life is important to me, in this philosophy, as they do something for me. They are pawns on my table in what they can give and do to satisfy me. My world is surrounded by me. People are important in what they can do for my values, my standards, my promotions. The "me-ism" philosophy circulates all around us today as many constantly look out only for # 1. It is seen, unfortunately, in politics, business, education, the prosperity gospel, many personal goals, lack of concern for the needs of the less fortunate around the world, exclusive religion, lack of compassion and gratitude, and me and my area of perspective as the only significant one at all times.

LISTEN FOR THE VOICE OF GOD

There are many voices crying to us in our land calling us to a way that is a lower way. But the voice of God is seeking to penetrate our very being, and we need to listen for it. Listen. It may be a still, small voice that comes echoing softly through the roaring noise of the other voices. But listen and see if you can hear it. It will whisper to you one thing for sure and say: "learn to speak clearly and distinctly." In an age of so much "gobbledygook" and double talk, do we not need to speak more plainly about the things of God and life? Do we not need people in politics and religion who will stand up clearly for what they believe? We can see what their stand really is, and we will either like it or not like it. We will either follow them or not follow them. I hope that adults and our young people will learn to speak plainly and distinctly in an age that avoids clear speech.

The Pentagon, which is not often noted for clear talk, put up a sign once which read: "This passage way is non-conducive for an indefinite period of time to traffic." What that sign meant was, "Keep out!" Why not just say it plainly and clearly? Some of you may have seen a number of years ago the movie, *The Graduate*. In that movie, a young man has just graduated from college, and he is confronting life with all of its uncertainties and mass confusions. In one scene he is in the swimming pool under water looking at the people who are all talking in a distorted way. Nobody is really making much sense. All the conversation seems to be nonsense.

The movie focuses on the need to communicate more clearly in an age of noise and confusion. We need more people who will speak clearly and distinctly.

THE CLEAR VOICE OF JESUS

Jesus Christ is the epitome of one who learned to speak clearly. They didn't crucify Jesus because they couldn't understand what He was saying. They understood very clearly what He was saying. The religious leaders knew that He was challenging their religion and their way of life. He was calling them to a higher way. The call to speak simply does not mean that you speak tritely. Deep meaning can be expressed simply without being trite. For something to be simple does not mean that it has to be simplistic. We need to learn to make the distinction between the two and learn to speak plainly and simply so people can hear us.

Once it was said of a preacher, who was noted for his theological abstract language when he preached, "I wonder if he talks to his wife like that?" We need people who will talk to us plainly about life so that we can hear the message that God is seeking to say to us. Listen to the voice of God as God seeks to guide us.

LISTEN TO THE VOICE THAT SAYS YOU ARE LOVED AND ACCEPTABLE TO GOD

I hope that you will also hear the voice that comes to you saying to you that you are loved and acceptable to God. Notice in the New Testament that Jesus told us that God comes searching for us even while we are sinners. We do not become sanctified, and then we become OK to God. God loves us even while we are sinful, and He comes seeking and searching after us to bring us back to Himself. Now that doesn't mean that God loves our sin. But God loves us as individuals and calls us to the very highest and best we can be with our own gifts.

I read recently of a hospital chaplain who said that at last he had gotten to the point where he could look into the mirror and say, "I like you." A lot of us don't like ourselves very much. We are too tall, too short, too thin, too heavy. We don't like this or that about ourselves. We have to learn to accept ourselves, and as Paul Tillich says, "accept God's acceptance of us." We are loved by God, and God cared for us so much that He came into the world to die for us. Hear the voice of God that comes to us and says to you," I appreciate you, I love you, and I want to guide you in life."

THE VOICE THAT CALLS US TO THE WAY OF INTEGRITY

Listen also for the voice of God that comes saying to us that He is a God of integrity, and He wants us to have high values in the way we live and walk. It is sad today to live in a world in which the trust level has fallen so low. We have seen its loss from cheating in middle school to corruption in Watergate by government officials. We have gotten to the point that we really do not know how much we can trust a commercial on television or how much you can trust an advertisement in the paper. Too often they do not live up to what they say they can do or will do. We find young people who participate in shoplifting or cheat in school. We hear about books that are stolen from public libraries. They had to put in new systems to protect the books. What has happened to our value system in our world today? Where is integrity? Where are those people who stand up for those things that are worthwhile, lasting, and meaningful? When is a person's word his or her bond? What has happened to our real sense of integrity and values? We need to hear God calling us to live a life of honesty, decency, and fairness in the way we relate to others.

General William Dean was taken prisoner in the Korean War. He thought he was going to die. He had been in prison for three years and before his capture had survived in the mountains for thirty-five days with little food. He wrote his family a letter thinking that it would be the last he would ever write to them. And he said something like this. "Mildred, I want to thank you for the twenty-four wonderful years that we shared together and I love you." To his daughter, June, he encouraged her not to delay making her mother a grandmother. Then he wrote directly to his young son, Bill. "Bill, remember that integrity is the most important thing of all. Let that always be your aim." Let us listen to the voice of integrity that calls us to the higher way than we have ever realized. Our call is not to give way to the lesser and base values in life.

THE VOICE OF DISCIPLINE

I hope that we will also listen to the voice that is calling us to a sense of discipline. Young Samuel had disciplined his life to respond to the call of his master. Discipline is an unpopular word today. So many people want freedom. They don't want any restraints or demands. They want absolute, total freedom. But absolute total freedom only brings anarchy. Those in life who have found the most lasting values have been those who have been able to discipline themselves. No one can ever become a musician without discipline. Nobody ever becomes a good athlete without discipline. Nobody becomes a medical doctor, attorney, dentist, etc., without discipline in his or her life.

We had a young man in a church where I was pastor who broke the state record in track for Virginia when he was in high school. He didn't get up one day and say, "you know, I think I want to be a great runner" and so he broke the record that day. Instead he got up day after day, week after week, year after year, and ran fifteen miles a day. He disciplined his body and mind to do that. No, he didn't start running fifteen miles the first day, of course. He built up to that. He ran and ran until he became one of the greatest cross country runners in the state. It came about because of discipline.

Jesus has told us that His way is narrow. The broad way that leads to destruction is the way without any kind of control, without any kind of restraints. But Christ calls us to a narrow way which demands discipline. But His way is always narrow. Love is narrow. It can focus on particular persons. When I read something, that means that I have narrowed my vision to that book or magazine. When I choose a vocation, I narrow it to that one. There needs to be some sense of discipline and control in one's life or we become totally chaotic without direction and meaning. I hope we can hear the voice of God calling us to discipline.

THE CHALLENGE BEFORE US

And like young Samuel, I hope we also can hear the voice of God as God calls us to a new challenge that lies before us. Samuel responded to God and met the challenge before him. Around the turn of the 20th century, the Director of the U.S. Patent office resigned. He said that all the great inventions had already been discovered. He thought that there would no longer be a need for his office. And this was around the turn of the century. Look at the inventions and technologies which have been discovered since then. Young people, the greatest books, the greatest music, the greatest discoveries have not yet been realized. Just look at what has happened in the last few years. The greatest dreams of what is going to be accomplished in space, in the ocean, in the environment, in medicine, in science, in technology, etc., are still waiting to be discovered.

There is a great, bold, exciting adventure lying before us, and I hope that you and I will not listen to the voice that says everything has already been done and accomplished. There is much left for you to do, because the greatest challenge is still ahead. In the areas of war, poverty, disease, and human relations, there are areas which challenge us. This is true in the scientific and literary fields as well. Many new worlds loom before us. Why do we settle for the present when the pull of the future is upon us? The greatest challenges still lie ahead, and I hope, adults and young people, that like Samuel, when you hear the voice of God, you will accept your responsibility and say, "Speak, Lord, for your servant hears." Respond like Samuel and do your task.

ACCEPT THE CHALLENGE

Several years ago, a football team was being absolutely stomped by its opponent. The score was sixty-four to nothing, and they were in the last quarter. The team that was losing had absolutely been beaten in every way by the stronger team. The coach put in a new tailback who was not battered. The quarterback received the ball, and then turned around and tried to give it to the player. He was chasing him in the backfield and trying to pass him the ball. The coach kept yelling from the sideline: "Give the ball to Callahan. Give the ball to Callahan." The quarterback finally hollered back and said, "But Callahan says he don't want the ball."

We are in a world in which there are many problems and a lot of challenges. I hope that you and I will not be like the young tailback and say. "I don't want the ball." The ball is now being passed into our hands. You and I have responsibility to do our· part in seeking to help overcome the problems in the world today. You and I need to rise up to meet the challenges that are there. The ball is in our court, and we are challenged now not just to be recipients, not to receive what others have done for us, but now we are challenged to be a part of the force that will make a difference in society as we seek to overcome and change some of the things in our world.

LISTEN TO THE VOICE THAT CALLS YOU TO THE HIGHEST AND BEST

There are many voices calling to us from all kinds of quarters today saying, 'walk in my path.' I hope that you will listen and determine that the true voice amid all the false voices is the voice that calls you always to the highest and best you can be. I hope that you will never settle for the given or the mediocre but will hear the voice calling you to be more than you are. I hope that you will hear the voice of God which is calling you to discipline your life and give it control and direction. I hope that you will hear the voice of God during all the confusion, corruption, crime, sin, lying, and cheating which says to you to stand up for integrity and decency. Let your word be a word that stands for truth and high values. I hope that you will hear the voice of God, echoing among all the voices around you, which says that you are loved and acceptable. This voice of God declares that you can be forgiven and that you can rise up as a new person to be God's son or daughter to live for Him in His world. Amid all the loud confusing voices, I hope that you can hear the whisper of the still, small voice of God calling you to come, follow Him. The Christ-like way is the only real abundant life. I hope you will not miss it because you have chosen the broad way instead of the narrow way. Listen. Listen. God is speaking. Let us hear God's voice and follow.

> *O Jesus, poor and abject, unknown and despised,*
> *have mercy upon me and let me not be ashamed to follow you.*
> *O Jesus, hated, calumniated, and persecuted,*
> *have mercy upon me, and let me not be afraid to come after you.*
> *O Jesus, betrayed and sold at a vile price,*
> *have mercy upon me and make me content to be as my Master.*
> *O Jesus, blasphemed, accused, and wrongfully condemned,*
> *have mercy upon me and teach me to endure the*
> *contradiction of sinners.*
> *O Jesus, clothed with a habit of reproach and shame,*
> *have mercy upon me, and let me not seek my own glory.*
> *O Jesus, insulted, mocked, and spit upon,*
> *have mercy upon me and let me run with patience*
> *the race set before me.*
> *O Jesus, dragged to the pillar, scourged and bathed in blood,*
> *have mercy upon me, and let me not faint in the fiery trial.*
> *O Jesus, crowned with thorns and hailed in derision;*
> *O Jesus, burdened with our sins and the curses of the people;*
> *O Jesus, affronted, outraged, buffeted,*
> *overwhelmed with injuries, griefs, and humiliations;*
> *O Jesus, hanging on the accursed Tree,*
> *bowing the head, giving up the ghost,*
> *have mercy upon me, and conform my whole soul*
> *to your holy, humble, suffering Spirit.*[2]
> (John Wesley)

---

2   Cited in *The Communion of Saints: Prayers of the Famous*, edited by Horton Davies (Grand Rapids, Michigan: Wm. B. Eerdmans Publishing Co., 1990), 100.

CHAPTER 2

ON SEEING AND
HEARING GOD

The five-year-old boy dropped his mother's hand which he had been holding so tightly, and he raced through the open door of the church sanctuary and began to look first behind the pulpit, in the choir loft, under the pews and beside the organ. He dashed from one spot to the other until his mother grabbed him and asked, "What are you looking for, Charles?"

"Why, I'm looking for God," he responded. "You said this was God's house. Where is he? I can't find Him!"

Like this small boy, many persons have searched for God in churches, on mountain peaks, by rushing streams, in the loneliness of a wooded forest, in quiet solitude, and under starlit nights. Some have traveled through strange lands, visited sacred places or talked to holy men and women. Others have blazed trails inward and studied scholarly books and the noble thoughts of others. This quest has carried some seekers around the world. Others, like this small lad, have cried, "Where is God? I can't find God."

In the midst of war, suffering, disease, famine, disaster, failure, death or grief, many wonder where God is. They long for a clear word of hope or encouragement. But sometimes heaven seems to be made of brass and does not respond to a cry of need. Like the author of Psalm 42, Job, Elijah, Jeremiah, and Jesus hanging on the cross, and countless others through history, including at times maybe you and me, many have longed to have a clear word from God. This has led some to question God's existence or pushed them to speak of the absence of God. But the seemingly silence of God does not prove the non-existence of God. The problem usually lies, I believe, in our mistaken, narrow, obscure, or childish concept of God.

IMAGES OF GOD

God is "a vague, oblong blur" to many. There is no definite meaning or image which some could use to describe God. Others hold images of God which are inadequate for a sound religious faith. God is a sweet, nice, easy-going old man, like Santa Claus, who will reward them if they are good. God is like a kindly grandfather who wants to make his grandchildren happy. God, then, becomes a sort of "divine bellhop," who exists to give people service. Our wish is supposed to be God's command.

Still others see God not as kind and beneficent, but as a revengeful, violent, vindictive type of personality, who demands a "pound of flesh" from men and women. God is seen as demonic and one who sends suffering, pain, horror and evil upon people. Christians through the ages have drawn upon this view of God to justify their bigotry, prejudice, empire expansion at the expense of the countries they have invaded, the massacre of thousands of Native Americans, the African slave trade, white supremacy, slavery and segregation, etc. This distorted concept, based on the Old Testament biblical writers' concept of a violent God, sees everything that happens as God's intentional will. These persons have never explored the meaning of free will with which God endowed creation, nor understand the teachings of Jesus about the God of love for all persons.

I want us to try to see through the dense fog, the frosted glass perspective, and the vastness of the subject matter; to see if we can peer through the darkness and sense the presence of God. In spite of all the arguments of the atheists against the existence of God, the bold absolutism which some assert about God on the opposite extreme and the sweet naiveté which is often declared in between these extremes, I still believe in the existence of God. I confess my timidity at trying to address such a subject. I hesitate, am reluctant, and tremble at the thought of speaking with such assurance about God. I also confess that what I say arises out of my own experience and my faith commitment to this God. In what is surely an impossible task, I want us to think about God under two themes: The nature of God and the work of God. I want to try to lift the curtain back slightly and see if we can see a little light about the God we worship.

I. THE NATURE OF GOD

Let us begin first by trying to explore the nature of God. As H. F. Rall has observed: "God is not one of our religious beliefs; he (sic) is *the* belief. He is not one doctrine; he is the heart of all doctrines."[3] The Bible does not attempt to prove the existence of God. God's existence is assumed. The writer of Genesis opens with the declaration, "In the beginning God created" (Genesis 1:1). Throughout the Bible, the writers announce the God they have experienced. There is no effort to demonstrate God's existence, but there is a recognition of who and what God is. Faith is a response to the God who has been heard and seen.

Mystery

Any attempt to speak about God causes one to stop at the edge of a great mystery. No one is able to throw open the door of heaven on a wide hinge and declare that he or she knows all about

---

3   Rall, H. F. *The Meaning of God* (Nashville: Abingdon-Cokesbury, 1925), 6-7. The following books have been especially helpful to me: Emil Brunner, *The Christian Doctrine of God*, (Philadelphia: The Westminster Press, 1950); William Newton Clarke, *The Christian Doctrine of God*. (Edinburgh: T & T Clark, 1912); Albert C. Knudson, *The Doctrine of God*, (New York: Abingdon Press, 1930); Wolfhart Pannenberg, *Jesus, God and Man*, (Philadelphia: The Westminster Press, 1968); William Temple, *Nature, Man and God*, (London: Macmillan & Co., 1956); Paul Tillich, *Systematic Theology*, Vol. I, (Chicago: The University of Chicago Press, 1951), Douglas John Hall, *Professing the Faith* (Minneapolis: Fortress Press 1993), R. Kirby Godsey, *When We Talk about God...Let's Be Honest* (Macon, GA: Smyth & Helwys Publishing, 1996), Jack Miles, *God: A Biography* (New York: Alfred A. Knopf, 1995), John Micklethwait and Adrian Wooldridge, *God Is Back* (New York: The Penguin Press, 2009).

God. No one really has the divine perspective. That would be an audacious claim. And I am not attempting that here in these words.

When I was a student in seminary, one of my professors had presented his view on a certain theological theme and then paused to see if any student had a comment. "Well, professor," one of the students declared quite seriously, "we have listened to your interpretation; let's look at it now from God's viewpoint."

But who can dare say that he or she has on God's glasses and sees God's viewpoint! There is no 800 number for direct dial or an email address to God for absolute information about God. Truth about God is always read with misty eyes or through glasses darkened by ignorance, superstition, or religious, economic and cultural mores. We always know less than we think about God and define our religious beliefs in terms that are less than they are; and yet more than we comprehend. We struggle to express what we really believe and confess that our words often conceal as much about God as they reveal.

Religious history is marked with some dark days when individuals dared to proclaim that they had the only and final insight into religious truth. From this bigoted and intolerant attitude came the Inquisition, Holy Wars, witch burning, Fascism and Nazism, denominational wars and schisms. There is no one more dangerous than the person who assumes to have the only interpretation about God.

As we strive to search for a belief in a "hidden" God, or seek to understand the mysterious God we worship, we can only use symbolic language to describe what we experience in this encounter. In the Bible, God has been pictured as a shepherd, king, judge, father, brother, rock, fortress and many other images drawn from human experience. Whenever men and women have tried to speak about God, they have utilized symbols, pictures and familiar images. We can only speak of the divine in terms that are meaningful to us. None of these images can exhaust or is adequate to depict the majesty and mystery of God. God is more profound than any of our most exalted words, images or phrases.

No matter how descriptive our terms are to describe the eternal God, they always fall short. God cannot be confined to our human pictures. Idolatry is the absolutizing our symbols about God. We are all like a small child peeping through a knothole in a fence to see what is on the other side. Our field of vision is limited and we get only a narrow glimpse of truth. We are like small children playing in mud puddles after a rain and assuming that they can see the whole world in the reflection of one of the puddles. All of our symbols only serve as pointers to God. God is far more than we can ever think, express or realize.

God is not limited to my knowledge or description or anyone else's perspective. No description is ever final or complete, nor is God confined or limited to our creeds or statements of faith. God cannot be imprisoned in the Bible, our creeds, theologies, religious institutions or organizational systems. Neither can God be confined to the images of our stained-glass windows or limited to any religious interpretation. The fresh wine of God's presence always shatters old wineskins.

An Arab philosopher was once asked how he knew there was a God. "I look outside my tent," he answered, "and I can tell whether a man or a camel has passed by the footprints." How do we see God? By the footprints. Our knowledge of God rests not by proofs but by parables, not by speeches but by signs, not by absolute phrases but by intimation clouded in subjectivity.

Holiness

The mystery of God's nature leads us next to speak about the holiness of God.[4] The most basic act of our religion is the worship of the Holy God. The holiness of God is what sets God apart from humanity. God's holiness is what constitutes the innermost nature of the divine. God's absolute purity and moral nature confronts

---

4   See Rudolf Otto, *The Idea of the Holy*, (New York: Oxford University Press, 1958).

men and women with our sinfulness and the demand for reverence. God must always be approached in a respectful and reverent way.

The holiness of God is stressed throughout the Scriptures. When Moses approached the burning bush, he was told to take off his shoes because he was on holy ground (Exodus 3:5). Moses had to bow in reverence before God would speak to him. Isaiah had a striking vision of the holiness of God and heard the angels declare: "Holy, holy, holy, is the Lord of hosts; the whole earth is full of God's glory" (Isaiah 6:1-13). God's holiness attests to the divine mystery (Isaiah 45:15).

The basic meaning of the word translated as holiness in the Old Testament conveys the image of "separation." Holiness is the distinguishing quality which sets God apart from humanity and all the rest of creation (Isaiah 40:25; 57:15; Revelation 4:8-11). Holiness denotes the moral perfection of God, the absolute and perfect moral excellence of God's being. To human beings, this exalted and sublime God is always, to use Luther's figure, *Deus absconditus*. Even in God's revelation to us, God is known only in a veiled form. Not only is God "the Holy One," God alone is holy. Holiness is a unique quality of the Author and Creator of all things. Kneeling in awe before our Creator, we can only declare: "Thou only are holy" (Revelation 15:4).

Holiness can be attributed to other things only as they derive their holiness from God. Places, objects or persons can be called holy only in the sense they are "holy (separated) unto the Lord." A temple or church is holy only because it is set apart to worship God. The Sabbath or the Lord's Day is holy because it is set aside for rest and the worship of God. The Bible is considered holy because it guides persons through its words to learn about and meet the holy God. Jesus taught His disciples to pray: "Hallowed be thy name" (Matthew 6:9). He was noting the holiness of God and that God's name is to be treated differently from all other names.

God's holiness means God is "wholly other." Our human sinfulness separates us from God. A great chasm separates us from God. No one can fully know God's thoughts or ways. God's holiness makes the divine nature incomprehensible (Job 11:3-12; Psalm 137:6; 1 Corinthians 2:11). God's holy nature is also incomparable. No figure, image, word or description is adequate to describe God fully. Words like fire, light, flame, brightness all fall short of depicting the wonder of God's holiness.

Many today have lost the sense of the holiness of God. They approach God in a far too familiar and unbiblical manner. They want to use very intimate words to describe God like "the Man Upstairs," "Mr. Big," "The Boss," "My Pal," a "Living Doll," or my "Bosom Buddy." They want God as a chum or a pal and have lost sight of the radical nature of God's holiness. God is not someone we can manipulate or control for our purposes, but the Holy One before whom we fall in awe and worship. Like Isaiah who met God in worship, we cry: "Woe is me! for I am undone, ... for mine eyes have seen the King, the Lord of hosts" (Isaiah 6:5). The holy, blazing light which reveals the gulf that separates us from God also reveals the bridge which crosses that chasm with God's redeeming love (Hosea 6:1-6; Isaiah 54:5; John 17:11).

Personal

The Bible affirms clearly that God is personal. It would be awful to worship an impersonal God like an Unmoved Mover, or a First Cause or a Principle of Order. Following the biblical model, I will not attempt to prove the existence of God, which I am not sure anyone can, but I begin with the faith affirmation that God does exist. Since all the philosophical arguments for the existence of God are based on something that is assumed to be true, they are not really "proofs" but pointers to help those who may in fact already believe. Belief in God, I am convinced, is not based on the conclusions of arguments but rest on experience. The various philosophical arguments may not convince us of God's existence, but they can help clarify our struggle to know God.

The question then is, if God exists, what kind of God do we worship? In the Bible the one true God is never seen as abstract or impersonal. God is One who communes with men and women. God is depicted as a personal being who speaks with man and woman. God is seen as the One to whom they can express their joys and concerns in prayer and be assured of being heard. Often the Old Testament uses anthropomorphic images to describe God. A primitive anthropomorphism which depicts God as bodily walking in fields and listening with physical ears, or getting angry, or getting tired, etc., is a clue to the biblical way of perceiving God as personal. God is not seen as an abstract force or an unknown cause in the Bible but is described as personal. God is addressed as "Thou" and speaks as "I" (Exodus 3:14; Psalm 23:4; Isaiah 4:4).

To describe God as holy, just, loving and righteous ascribes qualities to God that are only appropriate to a personal being. God's personal nature is implied in men and women's trust, dependence, fellowship, forgiveness and guidance of God. As far as we know, only persons can make moral choices, therefore, the fact that God makes moral choices presupposes that God is personal. Jesus' phrase, "Our Father" in the model prayer is addressed to a personal God.

The Scriptures present God as the ultimate reality upon which all the rest of creation depends. God alone is God. There are no other gods. The Bible affirms a monotheism in contrast to the pagan concept of numerous tribal or territorial gods. But this one God is a personal God who makes the Divine presence known to humanity and is concerned about the burdens and cares of all persons.

F. W. H. Myers, an English essayist, was asked once what one question, if he could, he would propose to the legendary "all-wise" Sphinx. He responded that his inquiry would be, "Is the universe friendly?" His question is the question of many. Is there a friendly God in control of the universe?

"Father" is a word that is often used to describe God. In the Old Testament, the fatherhood of God usually refers to the nation Israel as the elected child of God the Father. God as Father had "adopted" Israel and demands an obedient response (Exodus 4:22; Psalm 103:13; Malachi 1:6). Jesus used the name Father to address God. This word expressed his sense of a close and intimate relationship to God. He taught His disciples to pray, "Our Father" (Matthew 6:9). After the seventy disciples returned from their successful mission, Jesus prayed joyfully: "I thank you, O Father, Lord of heaven and earth" (Luke 10:21). In John 17, Jesus addressed God as "Father," "Holy Father," and "O Righteous Father." Jesus not only spoke of God as Father but as "my" Father (Matthew7:21; Luke 2:49). His use of "Abba" opened a totally new sense of intimacy (Mark 14:36). As He was dying on the cross, He prayed, "Father into your hands..." (Luke 23:46). The English New Testament scholar, T. W. Manson, observes that Jesus rarely spoke in public of God as Father but considered the fatherhood of God so sacred that it was reserved for His disciples who could understand His meaning of this usage.[5] Out of His own personal relationship with God the Father, Jesus sought to share this relationship with His disciples.

Let me pause at this point to stress that the use of Father as an image of God does not imply that God is masculine. God is not limited nor confined to human sexuality. God is neither male nor female, although I believe the Bible teaches that God's being contains whatever constitutes the essence of masculinity and femininity. When God is properly addressed, the pronouns he or she are inappropriate. Only "Thou" is correct.

In several places in the Scriptures, however, a feminine image is used to describe God.[6] In Genesis 3:21 God is described as a seamstress. In Isaiah 42:14 God says, "I will cry out like a woman in travail, I will gasp and not pant." In another place God states, "Hearken to me, O house of Jacob, all the remnant of the house of

5   Manson, T. W., *The Teachings of Jesus* (New York: Cambridge University Press, 1935), 98.

6   The following books offer guidance in this area: R. T. Barnhouse and Urban T. Holmes ed., *Male and Female*, (New York: The Seabury Press, 1976); Mary Hayter, *The New Eve in Christ*, (Grand Rapids: William B. Eerdmans, 1987); Leonard Swidler; *Biblical Affirmation of Woman* (Philadelphia: Fortress, 1979); Phyllis Trible, *God and the Rhetoric of Sexuality*, (Philadelphia: Fortress Press, 1978).

Israel, who have been borne by me from your birth, carried from the womb" (Isaiah 46:3). "Can a woman forget her sucking child," God asks, "that she should have no compassion on the son of her womb?" (Isaiah 49:15). A similar image is used later. "As one whom his mother comforts, so I will comfort you" (Isaiah 66:13). From the psalmist comes this beautiful image: "I have calmed and quieted my soul, like a child is quieted at its mother's breast" (Psalm 131:2). Psalm 123:2 depicts God as both master and mistress.

Jesus used a motherly figure for God when he stopped and wept outside the city as he made his last entrance into Jerusalem. "How often would I have gathered your children together as a hen gathers her brood under her wings, and you would not!" (Matthew 23:37). If God is depicted as a father who waits for his lost son in the parable of the prodigal son, isn't God depicted as the woman who sweeps her house until she finds the lost coins (Luke 15:8-10)? Since God is spirit (John 4:24), God cannot be limited to male or female images any more than we can limit God to the images of a father, shepherd, rock, fortress, judge, tower or king. Whether we use masculine or feminine images of God, each is meant to depict the personal nature of the Holy God. I personally believe that God as Spirit transcends the human sexual differentiation as masculine or feminine.

Love

Love is at the center of God's nature.[7] Too many persons have drawn upon the Old Testament writers' image of a violent and vengeful God depicted in such passages as Deuteronomy 7, 1 Samuel 15, Psalm 137: 9, and not the higher view in the Old Testament and especially in the teachings of Jesus and the New Testament. Brian McLaren has traced the devastating impact of the history of Christianity when Christians have followed the "genocide" con-

---

7   See Anders Nygren, *Agape and Eros*, (London: S.P.C.K., 1957); Daniel Day Williams, *The Spirit and the Forms of Love*, (New York: Harper & Row, 1968).

cept of God. In his book, *The Great Spiritual Migration*, McLaren summons us away from the belief in a God of domination and violence to a nonviolent God of liberation and love.[8] Richard Rohr is bold to declare that "I do not believe there is any wrath in God whatsoever—It's theologically impossible when God is Trinity."[9] In the Old Testament, the advanced view of divine love is expressed in several ways. The highest word for love is usually translated "loving-kindness" or "steadfast love." Often the word "faithfulness" is used with "loving-kindness" to denote that God is loyal and good, like a close friend. The idea of divine love was expressed in the covenant relationship between God and Israel. The pledge that God made with Israel was conditional upon Israel's obedience to God. Hosea was probably the first to present this high concept of God's love in the Old Testament.

One of the highest utterances in the Bible about God is found in the small epistle of John. There the writer declares, "God is love' (1 John 4:8, 16). Love originates from God and is centered in God's nature. All genuine human love has its source in God and is a reflection of that divine love. God's love is not a temporary expression of the divine nature, but is an eternal quality of God. God is eternal, and since God is love, God's love is also eternal and unconditional.

Everything God does is consistent with the divine nature of love. Love was the motive for God's act of creation. Through creation God expressed divine love for fellowship. God's creative love always desires the highest good for what God has created. Love was the stimulus for God's redemption. God was not content to let humanity suffer the consequences for their sins. Instead, God came seeking men and women to forgive them their sins. God's compassion, grace and mercy are expressions of this love. God has supremely revealed the depth of divine love in the life, teachings

8   McLaren, Brian D. *The Great Spiritual Migration* (New York: Convergent, 2016), 76ff.
9   Rohr, Richard with Mike Morrell *The Divine Dance: The Trinity and Your Transformation* (New Kensington, PA: Whitaker House, 2016), 140.

and death of Jesus Christ. God's patience, mercy, graciousness, for-giveness, and sacrificial love have been manifested in Christ. "For God so loved the world that he gave his only son so that everyone who believes in him may not perish but may have eternal life" (John 3:16). The New Testament boldly declares that the clearest evidence for God's love is seen in the gift of this Son in His redeem-ing sacrifice on the cross. "God commanded his own love toward us, in that while we were yet sinners, Christ died for us" (Romans 5:8). God's love is not limited to any one nation, race or group of people but is extended to all who will respond. The hymn writer Frederick Faber expressed that truth this way: "There's a wideness in God's mercy, like the wideness of the sea."[10] Wherever anyone responds to God's love, God is present.

God's love, as taught in the teachings of Jesus and in the rest of the New Testament, reveals that God is not vindictive, cruel, mean or demonic and must be placated. Rather than wanting to destroy men and women for their sins, God seeks persons out to forgive them and restore the broken relationship. God is not angry with humanity but loves the whole world and longs for its redemption. We know love because "God first loved us." (I John 4:19).

On one of Dr. Howard Thurman's trips to India, the noted minister and his wife had gone to bed when they heard a knock at the door. Dr. Thurman got up and went to the door and saw a young dark-skinned boy standing there. He could tell by his clothes that he was an untouchable. The young boy spoke in good English and said, "Sahib, Doctor, I stood outside the building and listened to your lecture. Tell me, please, can you give some hope to a nobody?"

The good news of the gospel about God is: Yes, there is hope for the hopeless. For those who feel broken and fragmented, Christ has come to give them love and life. The cross of Christ is the su-preme revelation of God's love for us. Christ has come to restore

---

10 Faber, Frederick W. "There's A Wideness in God's Mercy," *Hymns for the Living Church,* (Carol Stream, Illinois: Hope Publishing Co., 1974), 233-234.

broken relationships and set us right with God who loves us un-conditionally.

II. THE WORK OF GOD

The work of God is most clearly seen in what God does. The best evidence for what God is like is seen in the divine activity in the world. It is only in God's dealings with men and women and the rest of creation that God discloses what the divine Spirit is really like.

Creator

In many beautiful prose and poetic passages the biblical writers describe the world and its relationship to God. "The earth is the Lord's, and the fullness thereof; the world, and they that dwell therein. For he has founded it upon the seas, and established it upon the floods" (Psalm 19:1). The Genesis account opens with the sublime utterance: "In the beginning God created the heavens and the earth" (Genesis 1:1). There is no attempt by the biblical writers to prove God's existence. God's existence is presupposed. At the beginning of the world as we know it, God was present. Nothing existed before God and everything came into existence by God's action. The Hebrew word *bara* (create) in Genesis 1:1, 21, 27, is used in the Old Testament exclusively of God's creative activity. The biblical writers were not concerned with the question: How did the world begin? Their concern was with the God of history. God was known as a redeeming God within the history of Israel prior to being known as a creating God. Creation marked the beginning of history, and the God who made a covenant with Israel at an historical time is the God who created the world and was present when time began.

The biblical writers were not interested in the process of creation but that God was the creator. It is unfortunate that some persons try to make Christians choose between science and religion. The ancient pre-scientific view of the world presented in the Bible is not essential to the real message of the Bible. The biblical writers were not attempting to write books of science but were striving to present through mythological, parabolic and symbolic means deep religious insights. The purpose of the creation stories was not to write a textbook on science but to awaken men and women to their dependence upon God, the Creator, and their responsibilities to God (Deuteronomy 26:5-10; Psalm 24:1-2; 74:12-17). The first two chapters of Genesis and the other creation references in the Bible do not have as their purpose to write a description of the "how" or "what" of creation but focus instead on the "why" and "who." They were concerned with "why" there is a universe and "who" is sovereign. Science seeks to answer "how" the universe evolved or examines "what" is already in existence.

Science can explain how atoms behave but not why. It can give a description of how two molecules of sodium and carbon combine, but it is unable to say why. Science can show that quinine destroys malaria germs, but it cannot say why. There is an ultimate door through which science cannot pass. The biblical writers seek to answer the ultimate question, "why?" In powerful and ageless imagery, the writers say that God is the author and creative power who made the world. When one moves from the "how" of creation to the "why," he or she has moved from a scientific question to a religious one. Modern science has no more basis for judging the truth of religious convictions than has religion for forcing pre-scientific concepts on modern science.

For Christians, faith and science need not be in conflict.[11] What difference does it make if it took God millions of years to create the world instead of six literal days? In God's sight a thousand

---

11 Note especially Ian Barbour, *Religion in An Age of Science*, (San Francisco: Harper & Row, 1990); Emil Brunner, *The Christian Doctrine of Creation and Redemption*, (London: Lutterworth Press, 1955); C. A Coulson, *Science and Christian Belief*, (London: Fontana Books, 1961); Eric C. Rust, *Science and Faith* (New York: Oxford University Press, 1967); Francis S. Collins, *The Language of God: A Scientist Presents Evidence for Belief* (New York: Free Press, 2006.).

years are but a day. God may have worked through a slow evolutionary process for the development of nature and humanity. As a Christian, I acknowledge that God is the Creator and the source behind the evolutionary process. Human beings are not the product of blind choices but the product of the eternal God who may have used many methods to perform creative activity. Science uses evolutionary theories to explain the development of man/woman from a single cell to where we are today, but religion affirms that God is the Source behind this process.

When I was out west on vacation several years ago, I purchased as a souvenir a fossil fish from the Middle Eocene Period which is fifty million years old. This fossil is a reminder to me of the patience of God. God, the Creator, ever so slowly and patiently created the world. This fossil reminds me of the slow, evolving pace of our world, but I also affirm the God who is behind this process.

A college student once told his professor that he believed that the universe was nothing but a vast machine which made, repaired and ran itself. "Did you ever hear of a machine without a pedal for the foot, a lever for the hand, or an outlet for connection with some outside power?" the professor asked the student. The student replied that he had not seen such a machine. "Then," said the professor, "we had better not think seriously of the universe as a machine."[12]

God is indeed the Author and Creator of the world. Creation is not simply something that happened once-and-for-all at some moment in the distant past but is in some way continuous. God's activity in sustaining the universe is usually referred to as the providence of God. Whether one refers to God's control of the world as creative evolution or providence, the significant truth in both terms is that God has not deserted what God has created. God continues to guide, direct and care for the universe (Colossians 1:17; Hebrews 1:3).

---

12 Hazelton, Roger. *On Proving God,* (New York: Harper & Brothers, 1952), 95.

God is continuing to create. Even in divine rest God is still creating. God is creating in the movement of the planets and stars throughout the vastness of the universe. God is creating in the cycle of the seasons, in the new flowers, crops and grass, in the circulation of blood throughout the vascular system of our bodies. God is continuing to create in the birth of each newborn child, in the works that come from the minds of men and women in poetry, music, art, scientific advances, religious insights and in countless other ways. God is creating in the ability of the eye to pick up the words from this page and have them carried to our brains and produce thought and reflection. God is eternally creating and sustaining the world. "For of him, and through him, and to him, are all things" (Romans 11:36). (Note also Psalms 104; 139; Philippians 2:13; Matthew 5:45; 6:26-34; Romans 8:21-28). And as Jesus said, "My Father is working still and I am working" (John 5:17).

Revelation

"Show me how I can find God and I will believe," says the man. His voice is joined with many others who have longed to find God, to see God, to know God. Human beings are incurably religious. I believe the urge to see God is an impulse planted by the Creator. Centuries ago Augustine expressed this longing: "Thou has made us for thyself and the heart of man (and woman) is restless until it finds rest in Thee." (Note: John 1:18; I John 4:12; Psalm 42:1).

In our human quest for God, we discover that we "find" God not by our own initiative but by God's own self-disclosure. The God we seek is One who has already been seeking us and reveals the divine presence to us. God expects us to use our rational faculty in our quest for religious knowledge, but God is encountered not by discovery or inference from nature or some other source.[13] Our

---

13   See John Baillie, *Our Knowledge of God.* (New York: Charles Scribner's Sons, 1959), and John Baillie, *The Sense of the Presence of God*, (New York: Charles Scribner's Sons, 1962).

acquaintance with God arises out of a personal experience with the living God. Throughout the Scriptures, God is known to men and women through personal encounters—Moses by a burning bush, Isaiah in the temple, Elijah in a cave, etc. The revelation of God which these and other individuals experienced was a self-revelation of the divine personality. What God revealed to persons in this encounter was not ideas or propositions about God, but God. Persons met God. The content of revelation is God. As the revealer, what God discloses to men and women is God's divine presence. The revelation which the Bible affirms about God is not an object to a subject, but from subject to subject. Revelation is not concerned with giving information about God, but with the personal communion persons can have with the living God. Persons do not receive merely some ideas about God but the living God. God reveals God's presence to us. In that personal meeting with God, persons have learned what God is like. In God's immanence in the world, God is at work in the world whether we acknowledge that presence or not. Whenever God discloses the divine presence and persons respond, these persons, wherever they are, encounter God.

Revelation of God is personal not propositional. Our search ends not in believing *about* God but *in* God. As Paul attests, "I know whom I have believed" (2 Timothy 1:12). Although nature can be a medium of God's revelation, the unique revelation of God was made known in Jesus Christ. Here one sees the fullness of God's love and grace. Apart from the personal revelation of God in Christ, the terms "God's love" and "Jesus is Lord" have limited meaning. The meaning is given in and with the event itself. These are not static propositions that a person can arrive at by scientific methods, but truth which is learned in personal experience. Jesus Christ is certainly Lord eternally, but He becomes Lord to a person only when that individual commits his or her life in trust to Him in a loving encounter.

Knowing something about former President Obama is not the same as knowing him personally. You may know how tall he is, where he was born, what political party he belongs to, you may have seen him on television, or read about him. You may know all these things and more and still not know him personally. The same is true about God. A person may know numerous theological truths about God and still not know God personally.

The biblical view seeks to lead men and women to know God in a direct, personal encounter (Jeremiah 31:34; Colossians 1:12-20; Philippians 2:5-11; Hebrews 1:1-4). The biblical tradition stands in contrast to the tradition which seeks to establish God's existence by proofs or propositional beliefs. It calls men and women to a direct revelation of God through Jesus Christ. We, then, testify to what we have seen, heard, and experienced as the writer of 1 John 1:1-5 affirmed. Second-hand knowledge is not adequate for faith. First-hand knowledge arises out of direct experience from the self-disclosure of God. We know God because God first chose to reveal God's presence to us. In Jesus Christ God has made this presence fully known. "He that has seen me," Jesus said, "has seen the Father" (John 14:9).

Incarnation

The way God revealed the divine nature most clearly was through the Incarnation.[14] The best indication in the Scripture of the personal aspect of God's revelation is in the Gospel of John where the author writes about the Incarnate Word. The Word is not an impersonal term used to describe God's revelation but is John's expression to convey the fact that a personal manifestation of God was revealed when "the Word was made flesh" in the form of a specific man—Jesus Christ. The Incarnation is the central doctrine of the Christian faith. It is indeed the grand miracle of our religion. In Christ the interaction of divine and human are revealed in the One who is "both very God and very man." Christ not only revealed

---

14 The two most helpful books to me in this area are D. M. Baillie, *God Was in Christ,* (New York: Charles Scribner's Sons, 1948) and Jürgen Moltmann, *The Crucified God* (New York: Harper & Row, 1974).

something about God's nature to us, but he revealed what human life at its best could be when lived within God's will.

The Word seen in Jesus Christ has revealed to us what God is like. In a sense Jesus is the "picture frame" for our image of God. Through His life, teachings, death and resurrection, we see that God is not abstract, reserved, obscure, or immovable. Rather, like a shepherd seeking a lost sheep, a woman searching for a lost coin, or a father waiting for the return of his prodigal son, God's love reaches toward the sinner to win him or her back from their wandering or lostness. The Word did not become an idea, a theory or a proposition but it became a person—Jesus Christ. The Apostle Paul used such elevated terms to describe the Incarnation as "the image of the invisible" (Colossians 1:15) and "the fullness of God" (Colossians 2:9).

In response to Philip's request to show the disciples the Father, Jesus boldly declares: "Have I been with you so long and you still do not know me? Anyone who has seen me, has seen the Father" (John 14:8-11). Paul's phrase was "God was in Christ, reconciling the world to himself" (2 Corinthians 5:19). God's revelation took the form not of a written message but the form of a man. In Philippians 2:5-11, Paul presents one of the most beautiful hymns about the Incarnation found in the New Testament. Paul describes Christ as being in "the form of God" and emptying (*kenosis*) himself in humiliation and obedience to God the Father. The crucified One then becomes the exalted Servant (v.9) and before him "every knee should bow…to the glory of God the Father."

The mystery of God is no place more evident than in the Incarnation. God was uniquely in Christ, but Jesus was not the Father. Jesus prayed to God His Father and sought to follow God's will for His life. Nevertheless Jesus was divine. He communicated God's presence to humanity as no one else ever has. He was the Emmanuel—God with us. In Christ God focused the divine presence in a unique way. "The Word became flesh," John wrote, "and dwelt— pitched his tent—among us" (John 1:14). In the small book, *Jesus*

Is, Elaine, age eleven, said, "Jesus is the part of God you can see."[15]
We all need a part of God we can see, and Jesus Christ made God
visible to us. And the Word became flesh, and we could see God.

Redemption

As the central symbol of the Christian faith, the cross attests to
the redeeming grace of God.[16] The cross reveals the extent of God's
love. Although God is holy, almighty, righteous and eternal, the
inner nature of God's character has been summed up in the words,
"God is love" (1 John 4:8). The fatherhood of God has taken on
new content in the Incarnation of Jesus Christ. Through Jesus, men
and women have seen what God is like. God is like Jesus Christ,
who was kind, tender, loving, merciful, and caring. The cross is
the supreme sacrifice of love. The Incarnation and the cross reveal
God's identification with human suffering. The Incarnation led to
the cross, but it was completed in the resurrection. The cross reveals
the power of sin and grace and the resurrection reveals the triumph
of good over evil, hope over defeat, and life over death. How can
we measure the cost of the Incarnation and cross to God?

Who and what is God like? Jesus answered that question with
His life, teachings, and death. The eternal God is like the Son who
cares so much for lost children that God actively seeks them out
wherever they are. The parables of the lost sheep, lost coin, and the
lost son are word pictures that express the deep compassion and
eternal vigil of God (Luke 15:1-32).

The cross reveals the kind of love God has always had for
humanity. The cross makes apparent for all the world to see the
redemption which has always been in the heart of God. The Exodus

15 Johnson, Lenore. *Jesus Is,* (New York: Harper & Row, 1971), 3.
16 See Paul S. Fiddes, *Past Event and Present Salvation,* (Louisville:
    Westminster/John Knox Press, 1991); H. Wheeler Robinson, *The
    Cross in the Old Testament* (London: SCM Press, 1960); Vincent
    Taylor, *Jesus and His Sacrifice* (London: Macmillan and Co., 1951);
    William J. Wolf, *No Cross, No Crown* (New York: Doubleday &
    Co., 1957).

of the children of Israel from their bondage in Egypt shows the re-deeming character of God. The suffering servant in Isaiah 53 reveals the depths of God's suffering love. God did not become a loving God for the first time at Calvary. God has always been a suffering and loving God. *The Cross and the Old Testament* by H. Wheeler Robinson addresses the suffering and love of God as revealed in the Old Testament.

The death of Christ on the cross does not represent an isolated moment of God's love, but is a translation into history of an eternal fact about God's activity. The grace and love of God revealed in Jesus of Nazareth are the revelation of the eternal nature of the love of God who has always been seeking to make that divine grace known and acknowledged by men and women. Christ was "the Lamb slain before the foundation of the world" (Revelation 13:8). Jesus did not come to persuade God to be loving, but instead came to disclose the God who became incarnate to express this love for the world. The redemption of God does not reject God's creation. It fulfills it. The Creator is also the redeemer God. God's redeeming grace institutes a new creation.

Well, have you seen any signs of God's presence lately? The footprints of God are all across the pages of history. Those who have eyes to see, see. What sign would you accept? Some are like the man who said: "You say that God is *everywhere;* show me *anywhere* God has been. You say that God is *eternal.* Show me *any* moment that God has been with you."

There are persons who would dare to respond to that challenge. Abraham could point to the call that led him to leave his homeland and follow God into an unknown path. Moses might recount his experience by a burning bush that was not consumed from which he heard the voice of God. Jacob could relate a dream he had about angels ascending and descending on a ladder into the gate of heaven and struggling at Jabbok River with God. Isaiah was moved to awe in the temple by the holiness of God. Elijah sensed God's presence in "a sound of gentle stillness" outside a cave where he had fled in fright. Paul had a blinding experience on the Damascus Road with the risen Christ. Lydia, "whose heart the Lord opened" (Acts 16:14) in Philippi, became the first convert for Christ in Europe and the first member of the church in the West. Augustine responded to the quiet voice that instructed him to take up the Bible and read. In the midst of slavery and depression, Isabella, who came to be known as Sojourner Truth, encountered such love from God that she knew she would never be lonely again. Wesley's heart was strangely warmed in a small Moravian church. Lottie Moon had her religious experience rekindled in a college revival meeting and went to serve in China as the first single woman missionary appointed by Southern Baptists.

Countless others can point to a place and time when they had a sense of the presence of God. For me, it happened as a lad of sixteen while I was walking to church. The sense of God's call was unmistakable. My life has forever been different and my feet were set on a new path.

In *Children's Letters to God,* a small child writes:

> "*Dear God, Sometimes I think I can see you. I think I saw you last night. Is that a bad thing to say? I would like to very much. My mommy says you are always near us.*
>
> *Your friend, Herbert.*"[17]

God is always present, but like Elisha's servant our eyes need to be opened so we can see God around us. "God," Emerson says, "always enters by a private door into each individual." We all long for some clear sign. What sign would you accept? God's supreme sign was Jesus Christ. In Christ, the fullness of God has been made known. God came in a particular moment and place in history but continues to come through the Holy Spirit today. God is love. Let us open our eyes and ears that we might see and hear.

---

17   Marshall, Eric and Stuart Hample, Comp. *More Children's Letters to God* (New York: Essandess Special Edition, 1967).

CHAPTER 3

FACING TEMPTATIONS

The allure of temptation is everywhere. Temptations do not always come rushing into our lives with a devil or witch's mask. They may strut in with high heels in the form of a beautiful woman or may approach us in the guise of a handsome man. They may summon us when no one is looking or we think we can cheat and get by with it or steal and no one will know. The siren call of temptation may come on a bright and beautiful day and not on a stormy dark night, though either is possible. The enemy will likely not wear a black hat and make the evil choice obvious but depicts it in shades of grey and uncertainty. The temptation may summon us in a weak moment or in an area of our greatest weakness or beckon to us in what we assume is our greatest strength. No one young or old is immune to temptations. The subdued voice may appeal to us to forget about shame, project the matter on another, think of an alibi, rationalize, assume no one will know or care, note that it is just a habit, everybody does it or God will forgive us. "God after all is in the forgiving business," a voice whispers. Temptations still come with compelling faces even when we are older. I can attest to that. They may take new forms, shapes and disguises, but they still come.

ANOTHER POSSIBLE STORY

The temptations of Jesus appear in three of the gospels but not in John. (See especially Matthew 4:1-11). The order and wording is not the same in all of them, but the same basic message is clearly evident in Mathew and Luke. There is a slightly revised version which you may not have seen but would know. After fasting forty days in a wilderness place, Jesus, the hero of our story, became hungry and turned some flat stones into bread which satisfied His hunger. He saw many around him who were hungry and so He continued to transform stones into bread to feed hungry people. The people, of course, loved and admired him for it. Since he knew the positive response He had gotten from the people by this miracle, He performed another one by leaping from a great height and landing safely to the applause of all those who were drawn to Him for His great powers. In some unique way, He also brought political peace and prosperity to His followers for many years. After living to an advanced age with great wealth and security, He died and was buried in a grave to which thousands of His followers still return to pay their respect.

AN IMMEDIATE TEST

Hopefully, you know that is not the way the gospel story reads. Matthew and Luke indicate that immediately after Jesus was baptized by John the Baptist, He was led by God's Spirit into the wilderness, likely a sandy, hilly, limestone region between Palestine and the Dead Sea called Jeshimon. Why immediately? At His baptismal experience, Jesus had been anointed by the Spirit of God and words of approval were given to Him. For what purpose was He to devote his life? Now came His time of testing. Testing may be a more appropriate word for this experience than temptation. Could He really be the chosen instrument of God? The metal of His spirit would undergo the fires of testing to determine its quality. Would He pass the tests? The account of this episode had to originate from Jesus. No one else was there. Thus, this account is autobiographical. He had to have shared it with His disciples later or the gospel writers were producing it to present a lesson about the inner struggle of Jesus with His Messianic mission. This experience may also be representative of the continuous testing or temptation which Jesus had to compromise His mission. This confrontation with the powers of Satan was not a one-time event and then Satan slipped to the background for the rest of Jesus' ministry, but is symbolic of the struggle Jesus had throughout His ministry.

REAL TEMPTATIONS

Was the devil a literal physical personality that confronted Jesus in this wilderness experience? I, of course, do not know for certain. But I believe that is unlikely. I expect that Jesus experienced the powers of temptation the same way you and I do as an inner struggle within His own conscience. The gospel writers are clearly showing the human nature of Jesus in these temptations. As God's Son, He was still tempted like all people. The allurements of Satan appealed to His physical hunger, His desire for recognition and acceptance and His use of power. The Tempter tried to allure Him into yielding to a "short-cut" to reach His messianic goals. The author of Hebrews writes that Jesus "in every respect has been tempted as we are, yet without sin" (Hebrews 4:15). His temptations were not make believe or pretended ones, but were genuine tests of His commitment to His divine calling. The battleground was no less real because it was within rather than being external. The satanic seductions were personal ones for Jesus. Would or could He be faithful through all His personal struggles to compromise or yield to an easier or less demanding way to usher in God's kingdom? The forty days Jesus spent in the wilderness are a reminder of Moses fasting for forty days and nights (Exodus 34:28) and the Israelites being tested in the wilderness for forty years.

THE THREE TEMPTATIONS

The temptation story is depicted in a dramatic way with Jesus in a dialogue with the Devil in his sinister attempts to seduce Jesus into using a short-cut to reach His messianic goals or to turn in an entirely different direction and follow his, the Tempter's, leadership. The consciousness of Jesus' mission was affirmed at His baptism and following this grand affirmation Jesus was confronted by the cunning Tempter who questioned the meaning of this illumination of the Spirit and sought to compromise His vision of His ministry. The gospels set the wilderness place as the battleground for the drama between Jesus and the Tempter. "You just thought you heard the voice of God at your baptism," the Tempter suggested, "now listen to me and I will guide you in the *real* direction you should follow." "If you *are* the Son of God' (4:3), could be a way of planting doubt in Jesus' mind about what had happened at His baptism. But the Greek could allow the word "if" to be translated as "*Since* you are the Son of God." The Tempter's approach then was not to question Jesus' Sonship but to affirm him as God's Son and then to try and persuade him to see his mission in a more self-aggrandizing way. Let's consider now the three temptations.

THE TEMPTATION TO USE HIS POWERS SELFISHLY

"You are hungry," the Tempter observes. "See these flat stones around you. They look like bread. Why don't you turn some of those stones into bread and satisfy your physical hunger? You know you have that power as God's Son. Prove it. There is no need to be hungry." Jesus was being tempted to use his power in a selfish and personal way. He was tempted to satisfy his own personal needs with His miraculous powers. The temptation loomed larger; however, "If you satisfied your own "bread" need," the Tempter might be suggesting, "this could be a way to reach other persons as well. They have physical needs and you could satisfy their needs in a similar miraculous means. Use your powers now to satisfy your own needs and then later use your powers to 'bribe' people into following you when you satisfy their personal needs. Don't worry about their motives or why they desire certain things. Just give them what they want."

Jesus did not fall for the Tempter's trap. He responded with a quotation from Deuteronomy 8:3. "Man shall not live by bread alone, but by every word which proceeds from the mouth of God." Jesus reached back to Israel's wilderness experience and noted their dependence upon God for their provision. He refused to be a "bread Messiah" and use the wrong means to attract people for his kingdom. He faced this temptation later when he fed the five thousand by the Sea of Galilee with the lad's lunch of a few fish and loaves. The crowd wanted to make Him king after that miracle. (Matthew 25:31-46). Again, He refused to take a distorted way to draw people to His kingdom.

THE TEMPTATION TO USE SIGNS AND WONDERS

As the drama continues, Jesus is transported to the pinnacle of the temple, which may have been on a porch that rose four hundred and fifty feet above the Kedron Valley. "Leap from this height," the subtle Tempter urges, "and the people will follow anyone who can do such a wonder." Quoting Scripture, the Tempter reminds Jesus that "'God will command His angels concerning you,' and "On their hands they will bear you up, so that you will not dash your foot against a stone.'" (Psalm 90:11-12) The Tempter's suggestion is that such a sensational event will so dazzle the spectators that it will attract and win them to Jesus' cause. All doubters would have to be convinced after such an entertaining and wondrous sign. "Put God to the test," the Tempter seems subtly to muse, "and say that if God will do this spectacular thing for you then you will follow obediently." All of this was likely going on within the mind of Jesus, but here the gospel writer stages it as a live drama.

Jesus faced the choice of whether He was going to be a popular messianic figure who used entertainment and spectacular signs to win people to His kingdom or whether we would follow the way of the Suffering Servant that would lead to the cross. Again Jesus rebuffed the Tempter with a quotation from Scripture. "You shall not tempt the Lord your God." (Deuteronomy 6:16). Jesus knew that faith was not genuine faith that demanded assurance before one could say it was real. A faith that requires signs and sensational wonders could not be genuine. One spectacular event demands an ever greater one the next time around and an even greater one on the next occasion. One could not expect God to perform miracles to satisfy our desire to "prove" divine love and support. The signs and wonders that Jesus used later were not used to compel faith in His followers. He consistently refused to use them for that purpose.

(Matthew 16:1-4). Jesus refused to test His faith by putting God to the test. Jesus knew that faith was not a game saying: "God, if You will do this for me, I will do that for You." Real faith trusted God's promises without signs and even in difficult times.

THE TEMPTATION TO GAIN POLITICAL RULE THROUGH EVIL MEANS

The final scene in this drama is staged on a high mountain where the Tempter has taken Jesus and shows Him all the kingdoms of the world. "You have come to save this world" the Tempter asserts, "and look, here it is before you. Worship me and I will see that you get to rule it all." Satan knew how well that allurement worked. Had not many great leaders followed evil, forceful avenues to achieve their conquest? "Be the militant messiah that the Jewish people want. Forget this Suffering Servant stuff. No one wants a hurting, suffering messiah. They prefer a victorious, conquering figure who will overthrow their enemies with force and action. I can give you that leadership. Bend your ideals a little. Compromise your principles and let me show you an easier and less demanding way that still will lead you to your desired end." Did he suggest that Jesus might be another David or Judas Maccabeus or the new Zealot leader?

On this mountain top, not in a valley, Jesus confronted His dilemma: would He be a political messiah or the Suffering Servant Messiah? That was His choice now and throughout His ministry. Would He choose the way of comfort and ease or pain and suffering; acceptance and acclaim or rejection and the cross? He confronted that struggle in trying to get His own disciples to see that His ministry ultimately led to the cross. Words similar to what He would utter to the Tempter in a few moments were used to address Peter and the other disciples when they tried to dissuade Him from His sacrificial way of the cross. "Get behind me, Satan" (Matthew 16:22-23). Before He was arrested, Jesus struggled in prayerful agony in the Garden of Gethsemane about this same decision and prayed for strength to do His Father's will.

The allurement to make a deal with the devil has captured our imagination in plays like *Faust* who sells his soul for magical powers. Jesus knew the costly nature of this compromise. He also was aware that evil was not defeated by compromise or accepting facsimiles of God's created world or by making an alliance with evil itself. "Away with you, Satan!" Jesus asserts. "For it is written, 'You shall worship the Lord your God, and him only you shall serve.'" (Deuteronomy 6:13). Jesus refuses to compromise, use sensationalism, use His powers selfishly or bow His knee at the altar of the Evil one. He knew that this decision — this way — would lead ultimately to the cross and the path of the Suffering Servant. But He chose it with confidence and the assurance of God's presence.

CONTINUOUS STRUGGLE WITH TEMPTATIONS

The Gospel of Luke notes that the devil departed from Jesus after this period of temptations until another opportune time arose (Luke 4:13-14). This indicates that this was not the only time Jesus was tempted. His struggle with the forces of evil continued throughout His ministry all the way to the cross. In the Upper Room when Jesus observed the Passover meal with His disciples, He acknowledged that His disciples had stood by Him in His trials (Luke 22:28). The power of God's Spirit was with Him throughout His struggles. When Jesus had come to the fork in the road for a choice of direction in His ministry, He chose wisely. But the struggle was not over in the wilderness. It met Him everywhere He went in different shapes and disguises. In his novel, *The Last Temptation of Christ,* Nikos Kazantzakis portrays Jesus, while hanging on the cross in an instantaneous flash, being confronted by the temptation in these last hours to abandon the cross and live out his life as a normal man who is attracted to and wedded to Mary Magdalene, fathering children and living to a happy old age.

A QUESTION

"I understand how that relates to Jesus' temptations," you might say, but you ask: "What have these temptations to do with me? I have never been tempted to turn stones into bread or anything else. I have never been tempted to jump off our church's steeple. And I have never been shown all the nations of the world and told I would rule over them if I would worship the devil." In fact some of you might say:" Look ... I have trouble even believing in a devil much less that he would offer me the whole world! So, what's this passage to do with me?" That is a good observation. So, can the temptations of Jesus really relate to us in any way? Let's turn in that direction and see.

A MODEL FOR OUR RESPONSE TO TEMPTATIONS

I believe the response of Jesus to these temptations can offer us guidance in confronting our own battle with temptation. Jesus' response is a model for us. He, of course, was battling to determine His messianic direction and whether He would succumb to "short cuts" to reach His desired goal. We, too, face our temptations in a similar way and have to decide whether we will choose a path that is less than the high road in our journey through life.

THE TEMPTATION TO SELFISHNESS

The Tempter appealed to Jesus to meet a personal, selfish need by feeding Himself when He was hungry by turning stones into bread. Our "bread" temptation can take a variety of forms to satisfy our many physical or psychological needs. Too often we fall prey to our immediate desires without regard to the consequences it might engender. Our concern is to satisfy our wishes. Excuses fill our mind to justify why it is OK to do whatever we may know is wrong. C. S. Lewis in *The Screwtape Letters* has a senior devil advising a junior devil to keep a person's mind off the true and false nature of the temptation with such expressions as "It was a phase"

— "I've been through all that" — and don't forget the blessed word — "adolescent."[18] We are all too familiar with our many excuses for choosing the wrong over the right. I don't have to enumerate them all for you.

To live by bread alone is not merely the substituting of material values for spiritual ones. It is the way we often misuse our relationships to manipulate people for our own ends; twist information to meet our selfish ends; distort facts to justify our self-serving intents; satisfy our selfish appetites rather than seeking to meet human need; avoiding just and fair treatment of others when it might cost us inconveniences or loss of wealth or fame or personal reward; taking short cuts that hurt others so we can fill our own coffers; seeking immediate satisfaction rather than seeking to trust God for the reward that comes from patiently waiting. It is to assume that ultimate values are derived in material and physical means like possessions, fame, prestige, wealth, appearance, power or control. It is a hunger that is rewarded or satisfied only in selfish or physical ways.

Years ago, when W. O. Carver was a professor at the Southern Baptist Theological Seminary in Louisville, Kentucky, he used to give his students an interesting piece of advice when they were doing some pastoral counseling. "Young men," (and in his day there were only men in his class) he would caution, "If you are counseling a woman and you feel in the course of your counseling an attraction for this woman, excuse yourself for a moment and go into the next room and take your walking stick and hit yourself as hard as you can on the ankle. That pain will distract you for the moment, and then go back into the other room and say to the woman, 'You know I believe I need to refer you to someone else for further counseling.'"

Maybe what we all need in our times of temptations is "a walking stick" of some kind that we can use to strike our conscience to remind us of the proper perspective. To allow our selfish or physical

18 Lewis, C. S. *The Screwtape Letters* (London: Fontana Books, 1956), 52.

desires to dominate our thinking is to feed on bread that leads to
our spiritual starvation. We make the mistake of assuming that our
temptations will always confront us at our weakest point. Whereas
in reality they may surprise us by confronting us at what we assume
is our strongest point. Our descent down the "bread" path may not
be marked with signposts or by a sudden descent into evil ways
but may be a gradual path that slowly and quietly bears us away
at our strongest point to pull us down into the abyss. Our pride
in our religious convictions or self-righteousness may become the
unexpected labyrinth where the Tempter finds entrance.

A young man was trying to rationalize with an older mentor
why he had caved in to a temptation to compromise his values in
a business decision. "You cannot imagine the external pressures to
make that decision," the young man exclaimed. "But where were
your internal braces?" the mentor asked the younger man. We all
must have those internal "braces" or "walking sticks" that enable
us to resist temptations. We need to fortify our inner self with high
values, healthy and positive thoughts over negative and derisive
ones, and the sustaining power of a moral conscience that will expel
immorality and deceptions, and the abiding presence of the Spirit
of Christ who strengthens us to overcome evil with good. We need
to enrich our inner self with the awareness of the Apostle Paul's
claim that "No testing has overtaken you that is not common to
everyone. God is faithful, and he will not let you be tested beyond
your strength, but with the testing he will also provide the way out
so that you may be able to endure it." (1 Corinthians 10:13)

THE TEMPTATION TO PROVE GOD BY SENSATIONALISM

The Tempter had challenged Jesus to test God to see if God
would rescue Him in a sensational way as He leaped from the
high pinnacle of the temple. Before you dismiss this temptation
as being irrelevant to your life and mine, we need to see how we,
too, might face similar testing. Too often before we realize it we

have demanded of God some kind of sign or miracle. "If only God would make His presence clear to me, I would believe or know He was real," we say. "All I want is some kind of sign. Any kind would do." "Oh God, if You will let me get well," we implore, "I will give a thousand dollars to my church." "Let me not get caught this once, oh God," we argue, "and I promise I will never do it again." When I was in college, I had the opportunity to be a summer missionary to Hawaii. As I was being considered for the position, I prayed the following prayer: "Lord, if you will let me go as a summer missionary, I will become a full-time missionary." That was putting God to the test. I was selected to be a summer missionary to Hawaii but I did not become a career missionary. In my search to follow my calling, I gradually learned the perversity of my prayer. I soon realized that I could not bargain with or test God. God had a purpose for my life, but it would not be determined by trying to manipulate or test God.

Another way of trying to show God's approval is to claim that one's success or financial prosperity is due to one's favor from God and being one of God's chosen. Some voices in our land and on other continents are proclaiming a "prosperity gospel." "God wants us to be rich and successful," these voices affirm. Jesus is seldom the model for living but Bill Gates and Wall Street are lifted up as beacons along Life's way. In this philosophy of life, a Believer is expected to be rich. That is a sign of God's favor. If you are not rich and successful, then God's hand is not on you. "The truly faithful are blessed with prosperity," they assert. How anyone reconciles this with Jesus' call to "forsake all and follow Him" I do not know. This cheap prosperity gospel denies Jesus' call to bearing one's cross and following Him in sacrificial service. Some fine Christian people are wealthy and often use their financial resources to help others and to spread the gospel. But these persons refuse to claim special favor from God or that God has given them a special miracle so they could be rich.

Unfortunately, some people try to use religion-in particular the Christian faith- to gain power and control over others. Decades ago, Charles Dickens recognized this problem and wrote about it in his *A Christmas Carol* where Scrooge is presented in all his self-centeredness and unconcern for the poor and needy. The Ghost of Christmas Present addresses those who misuse religion to achieve power. "There are some upon this earth of yours who lay claim to know us, and who do their deeds of passion, pride, ill-will, hatred, envy, bigotry, and selfishness in our name, who are as strange to us and all our kith and kin as if they had never lived."[19] Even those who claim to be religious may often misuse, abuse, distort, deny or misunderstand genuine religion, especially the Christ-like way.

The contemporary church is often tempted to win followers by sensationalism. If we can entertain people, the churches will grow and the money will come in. Many of these churches are primarily consumer based. They appeal to selfish instincts. Whatever a person desires, wants, or needs, these churches seek to furnish so they will flourish. Worship becomes "show business." Instead of focusing on the God who is high and lifted up, these churches appeal to showmanship and entertainment. Sinclair Lewis' novel *Elmer Gantry* depicted a corrupt, showman-like religious preacher in the early part of the last century. Unfortunately, Gantry does not appear to be merely fiction today. His shallow, opportunistic, materialistic, ostentatious, superficial religion has found flesh in many of our churches today; Crowds are drawn to this perverted form of the faith which offers them prosperity religion, cheap grace, no responsibilities, entertainment, and their wants and desires are met in programs and activities for all ages. Most of these churches refuse to challenge their followers to take up Jesus' cross and follow Him in discipleship. They often toy with theology and offer a cut-rate religion at a bargain price of a little contribution. There is no call to confront the great social evils of crime, corruption, war, racism and bigotry. They offer peace of mind and possibility thinking to assure their listeners of ease, comfort and security without any reminder of the difficulty often found in following Christ.

---

19 Dickens, Charles. *A Christmas Carol, The Chimes, and the Cricket on the Hearth* (New York: Barnes & Noble, 2004), 51.

In Dostoevsky's famous novel, *The Brothers Karamazov*, a moving scene is set in Seville, Spain during the Inquisition. A figure that many believe is Jesus has been going among the poor and desperate people healing their diseases and moving among them with compassion. The Grand Inquisitor has this figure arrested and goes into his prison cell to speak with him. He asked "Is it Thou? Thou?" But receives no answer. He continues: "Don't answer, be silent. What canst thou say, indeed? I know too well what Thou wouldst say. And Thou hast no right to add anything to what Thou hadst said of old. Why, then, art Thou come to hinder us? For Thou hast come to hinder us and Thou knowest that. But dost Thou know what will be tomorrow? I know not who Thou art and care not to know whether it is Thou or a semblance of Him, but tomorrow I shall condemn Thee and burn Thee at the stake as the worst of heretics…" The Prisoner continues to remain silent, but suddenly, he approached the Grand Inquisitor in silence and softly kissed him on his bloodless aged lips. That was the only answer he gave. Then the Grand Inquisitor went to the door and opened it and said: "Go and come no more… Come not at all, never, never!" And the Prisoner went away.[20]

Does the modern church expel the living Christ by its rejection of His way, for the way of sensationalism and the prosperity gospel? Have we traded the cross for comfort and ease? The church seems at times so determined to grow and be successful that it will sell its soul to reach its goals. I honestly do not believe that most churches really want to deny their Lord or reject His way. They genuinely want to follow Him and serve Him. But do all of these ways that focus on comfort, peace of mind and prosperity not conflict with His way of discipleship? "The last temptation is the greatest treason;" penned T. S. Eliot, "to do the right thing for the wrong reason."[21]

---

20 Dostoevsky, Fyodor. *The Brothers Karamazov* (New York: International Collectors Library, n. d.), 230, 241.

21 Eliot, T. S. "Murder in the Cathedral," Part I, *Complete Poems and Plays of T. S. Eliot* (New York: Harcourt Brace Jovanovich, 1952), 196.

THE TEMPTATION TO WORSHIP AT THE SHRINE OF EVIL

The temptation which Jesus had to comprise His goal and worship Satan to achieve His mission was one He continuously confronted throughout His ministry. He was beset on many sides with the temptation of whether He would be a political messiah or the Suffering Servant. He had to make that choice. You and I do not have to face that momentous decision in our own choices, but we constantly face decisions that deal with various forms of compromise. We often have to make decisions that force us to choose between the higher and lower, the good or the better, the right or the wrong, less than our best, mediocrity or our best, compassion or detachment, love or unconcern, hope or despair, love of God or love of the world.

Our temptation may be to follow the Prince of Peace and Light or the Prince of Darkness and Confusion. The promise of the Christ does not always promise us comfort and ease but sometimes demands sacrifice and commitment to high moral values; while the devil may pretend to offer security, wealth, fame and recognition. The choice is not always easy nor without the risk of compromise. The offer to receive world recognition and authority is a drive that all of us recognize in ourselves. Will we choose to love the material values of the world which the Tempter offers or to love the spiritual values of the Kingdom of God which Christ offers? We must choose almost daily, sometimes hourly.

I know a business man who was told by his boss that he would have to make a transaction which he knew was illegal. Refusing to follow his boss's direction would cost him his job. He resigned rather than being dishonest. Would you or I have done the same? I know a high school athlete who was told by his football coach that he would have to play "dirty" if he was to be on the school team. He refused and quit the team. Would we have done the same? I know a young woman who was told that she could advance in her company only if she would give her boss sexual favors. She quit and reported him to superiors. Would we have done the same? Many are willing to sell their soul or forfeit their principles for success, recognition, wealth, advancement, fame or for some form of worldly authority or acknowledgement.

Sometimes our basic sin may not be selfishness or pride but, as Harvey Cox reminds us, it is apathy or "acedia" — indolence, laziness, or sloth. "Apathy is the key form of sin in today's world," Cox asserts.[22] Too often we don't want to get involved to help others in times of need; or want to take the time to show support; or simply feel too busy to be concerned about anyone else. We stand back and leave the responsibility for whatever need or concern that lies before us to someone else whether the problem is racism, poverty, pollution, homosexuality, immigration, refugees, religious liberty, political corruption, or some other issue. As a Christian, Christ challenges us to be involve and not stand on the sidelines and ignore the problems around us. Often the problems seem too immense and the solutions elude us, consequently we remain idle and wonder where God is. "God is present in the world, whether or not we happen at this moment to feel his presence in our hearts," Cox declares. "We do not carry him to the world somehow previously devoid of his presence. We meet him as he calls us to him in the world where he is already."[23]

When I was a teenager and leaving home on a date or to be with some of my friends, my father would often say to me: "Remember who you are!" I knew what he meant. His reminder was a summons to live wherever I went by the high moral values and Christian principles I had been taught. When we are tempted to kneel at the Tempter's throne of compromise, indifference, apathy, and material values, remember to be loyal to the royal way of Christ. Draw on the inner presence of Christ to resist the temptation to go down the wide road that leads to destruction. The real God we worship will be revealed in the choices and values we

22 Cox, Harvey. *On Not Leaving It to the Snake* (New York: The Macmillan Company, 1967), xvii.
23 Ibid., 98.

choose in our time of temptations. Will it be to walk the path of the Tempter who offers us material values only or the road of the Christ who lifts before us a light to guide us in the way of righteousness and high spiritual values?

CHARACTER FORMATION

Wayne Oates in his helpful book, *Temptation,* declares that the function of temptation is for the formation of character. "Temptation," he says, "is the crucible of human character formation."[24] Our response to the struggles we have with temptations throughout our life determines our path to growth. We learn from our temptations and strive to remain "steadfast" with Christ who strengthens us in our conflicts with them.

> Temptation is the testing ground between the strivings of the image of God in us and the strivings of our desires to be the masters of our fate, the captains of our souls, between the callings of our spirits and the claims of our biological destinies as human beings. The latter claims are the sources of our freedom and willingness to commend our spirit into the hands of God. To be given that freedom and willingness is the source of our serenity.[25]

Self-deception, Oates believes, is the "parent evil" of all temptation.[26] Temptation begins within ourselves, within the desires of our own heart or motives. Through prayer, nurtured in the Scriptures, striving for personal integrity, and a strong sense of purpose, and an inners sense of the Spirit of Christ's presence with us, we can find the strength to remain "steadfast" in the times of "testing." The Apostle Paul reminds us "No testing has overtaken you that is not common to everyone. God is faithful, and he will not let you be tested beyond your strength, but will with the testing he will

---

24   Oates, Wayne E. *Temptation* (Louisville: Westminster John Knox Press, 1991), 14.
25   Ibid., 103.
26   Ibid., 18.

also provide the way out so that you may be able to endure it." (1 Corinthians 10: 12-13)

THE DOOR OF LIFE

Franz Kafka tells the story of a man who approaches a door-keeper before a door marked "Before the Law." He seeks admittance to go through the open door but is told that he cannot be admitted at present but may be admitted later. The man looks inside the open door and notices that the doorkeeper is standing to the side of the door and picks up his bag to enter. As he moves forward to go through the doorway, the doorkeeper laughs and says, "If it tempts you so, then try entering despite my prohibitions. But mark: I am powerful. And I am only the lowest doorkeeper. In the hall after hall stand other doorkeepers, each more powerful than the last." The man then backs away and decides not to try to enter but remains by the door for years until he grows old. Knowing that he does not have long to live, a question comes to him and he asks the doorkeeper before the open door why no one else who strives to reach the law has not come to go through this door in all these many years? The doorkeeper, knowing that the man was approaching his death and was now hard of hearing, bellowed at him: "No one else could ever have been admitted here, since this entrance was intended for you alone. Now I am going to close it."[27]

An open door will stand before us as we journey through life, and as we seek to go through that doorway, we will encounter many strong doorkeepers, many stronger and more alluring than the last, but if we do not dare to enter our doorway we will miss our opportunity to find life. Choosing not to decide is to decide. In our journey through that doorway we will encounter the temptation of the one who rules the Darkness or the "temptations" of the Christ, who rules the Kingdom of Light. We have to choose to whom we will give our allegiance. What will be your choice?

---

27 Kafka, Franz. *The Metamorphosis and Other Stories* (New York: Penguin Books, 1992), 148-149.

CHAPTER 4

SEEKING DIVINE GUIDANCE

Most Christian persons with whom I have talked have indicated at some time or another that they want to feel like they have a sense of direction from God in their lives. Few persons, who are Christians, really want to say, "I am living in opposition to what I think God wants me to do." Most Christian persons want to say, "I feel like my life is within the will of God."

The big problem, however, is determining what God's guidance is. I wish I could tell you that it has always been easy for me to discern God's guidance. There have been times that I wished I could pick up the telephone and dial direct or send a text and say: "Hello God, this is Bill. I have a problem. Would you please tell me what to do?" But I have to tell you very honestly that I have never had a telephone call from God or a text message. I have never heard an audible voice telling me what to do. I have not had visions in the night that have instructed me plainly and clearly what I was supposed to do. To be candid, I have a problem with those who claim that they have had such experiences. Not many make such claims, of course. But a few do.

So, how do we get guidance for the future? Why, you know! Many turn to Ouija boards, crystal balls, fortune tellers, tea leaves, cards, horoscopes, and astrologists. Do we find directions from the stars? Where do we go for guidance in making decisions for life? I wish there were a machine labeled "Divine Guidance." The instructions might read: "Put your question in the slot, push it in, and out will come the divine answer." But it just isn't that simple, is it?

TRUST IN THE LORD

Yet the writer of the Book of Proverbs asserts, "Trust in the Lord with all your heart and he will direct your path." (See Proverbs 3:5-6). An ancient rabbi, Bar Kappara, stated that this text is the "hinge" on which all the essential principles of Judaism rest.[28] Trust in God is the hinge on which most of our life really does depend. This is a text which many of us have memorized since childhood. The call to trust here is for those who already believe in God. It is not addressed to those outside the faith but those who are within.

"Trust in the Lord with all of your heart, but lean not upon your own understanding." Ah, that's the rub, isn't it? Some of us lean too much upon our own understanding. The injunction "to trust in the Lord" would not be necessary if everyone did. The idolatry of self arises from those who puff themselves up and feel they have enough insights to make all the necessary decisions regarding life without any divine guidance. They feel no sense of dependence on God or on others. They feel sufficient in their own abilities. Probably one of the most blatant declarations of this kind of self-sufficiency was made by William Ernest Henley in his *Invictus*:

> *Out of the night that covers me,*
> *Black as the Pit from pole to pole,*
> *I thank whatever gods may be*
> *For my unconquerable soul.*
> *In the fell clutch of circumstance,*
> *I have not winced nor cried aloud:*
> *Under the bludgeonings of chance*
> *My head is bloody, but unbowed.*
> *It matters not how strait the gate,*
> *How charged with punishments the scroll,*

---

28 "The Book of Proverbs," *The Interpreter's Bible,* vol. IV, (New York: Abingdon Press, 1955), 799.

I am the master of my fate:
I am the captain of my soul.[29]

Here is an individual who feels self-sufficient. He declares that he has no need of God or, it would appear, even for other people.

THE VASTNESS OF THE UNIVERSE OBSCURES OUR IMPORTANCE

Go a step further with me into our theme and we encounter those who say that the vastness of the universe makes it impossible for us to be known. "How could there be a God who is concerned about us on this tiny speck in the universe?" they ask. Light, traveling at 186,000 miles per second, takes fifty million years to reach our planet from a distant star. One astronomer speculated that if God told an angel to go to the earth, that would be like telling a child to go to a sandy beach and pick out one particular grain of sand. The universe is so vast, these persons assert, that it would be impossible for God to know us or understand our needs. For these persons all this talk about God knowing individuals and their particular needs is difficult to believe.

SOME ASSERT THAT SUFFERING DENIES GOD

Others throw up a warning flag which points to the accidents, suffering, and pain in our world. To these persons, the enigma of suffering denies the love and providence of God. The tragic accident where twenty-seven young people were killed when a drunk driver ran into a church bus is evidence enough for them. They point to the suffering and pain all around us and assert that wars, suffering, accidents, and difficulties indicate that there is no divine power guiding our lives. Our lives are merely "floating" through

29 Henley, William Ernest. "Invictus," *English Literature: A Period Anthology*, edited by Albert C. Bough & George Wm. McClelland, (N Y: Appleton-Century-Crofts, Inc., 1954), 1407.

the universe, like the rest of matter, without any One who cares what happens to us.

IMPOSSIBLE TO COMMUNICATE WITH GOD

Still others declare that even if there is a God, we can't really communicate with God. "Why," they laughingly declare, "we can't even talk to each other." One of our biggest problems is understanding each other. How can we talk about communicating with God? Oh, now I know, there are some people who drive down a street and claim that God finds a parking place for them. Others claim that God has instructed them to telephone or text somebody, or has instructed them in some minute detail. I must confess that I am troubled by people who act like they have such a glib, bosom-buddy relationship with the eternal God of the universe.

ACKNOWLEDGE GOD

Well, when we lean upon our own understanding, it does seem to make for some tough going, doesn't it? Nevertheless, this ancient writer instructs us, "In all your ways acknowledge him (God), and he will direct your path." The word "acknowledge" or "trust" is a rich Hebrew word whose root meaning is "to see" or "to know." This word involves much more than just physical vision or intellectual knowledge, though that is a part of it. This is knowledge in its totality. This knowledge encompasses the heart, will, and mind. It is similar to Jesus' declaration of loving God with all your heart, soul, mind, and spirit. When you and I acknowledge God with all our capacity, then God's direction will be clear.

If we acknowledge God with all our heart, we will be humble. In the immensity of this universe, with all the questions and problems we encounter, who among us can act like he or she has infallible answers to everything in life? In humility, we bow our knee before God, as a small creature in this immense universe, and we acknowledge with gratitude our dependence upon God. We do not claim arrogantly to have all the answers or some special relationship with God that nobody else can possibly have.

NATURE LIVES IN HARMONY WITH GOD

If we acknowledge God with all our heart, we will also seek to learn to live in harmony with the universe like the rest of nature does. Man or woman in some way is in disharmony with nature, because we have so asserted our will that we have violated the natural order. In choosing to run counter to nature, man or woman has brought about pollution and all the other environmental problems that threaten our existence today.

When we study nature itself, we see how the other creatures which God has created live in harmony with God. An ant, traveling from its home, leaves a tiny chemical trail so that it can always find its way home. Through light beams which it emits, an ant can also find the shortest path back home. Mammoth butterflies migrate thousands of miles to reproduce. Salmons swim upstream following a chemical sensitivity within them, to find their place of origin to reproduce again. Birds migrate thousands of miles, because there is a homing instinct within them that pulls them back toward the place where they were born. These creatures live in harmony with the universe. God has created us to live in cooperation with Him in His world. Our self-centeredness both physical and spiritual has caused discord with God, within us, and our world. Rather than letting God guide, rule or direct us, we live in violation rather than harmony with God.

GOD GIVES FREEDOM TO HUMANITY

When we acknowledge God in all our ways, we discover, paradoxically, that in our dependence on God, God also gives us freedom. We are often disturbed by tragic accidents or suffering in our world. We sometimes forget that God has not made us like robots or pawns on a chess board. God gives us freedom to think and act. God gives us freedom to be successful or to fail, to win or to lose, to grow or shrink, to drink and become drunk or to remain sober.

God has created our world with the possibility of accidents, because God has given us freedom. Without freedom, we would not be authentically human. God does not want or will tragic accidents like the one where twenty-seven people were killed. But to become full human beings there must be freedom.

TOTAL COMMITMENT

If we acknowledge God with all our hearts, there will be a commitment of our total self to God. The ancient wisdom writer uses the word "all." "In all of your ways acknowledge him." The emphasis on all acknowledges our absolute dependence on God. It is a declaration that we are not sufficient by ourselves. Our commitment affirms our desire that God "lead us," "give us," and "guide us." We cannot acknowledge Him without kneeling in trust before Him.

The poet, William Cullen Bryant has stressed the guidance of God in the natural world which points to His plan for us as well in "To A Waterfowl."

> *He, who, from zone to zone,*
> *Guides through the boundless sky thy certain flight,*
> *In the long way that I must tread alone,*
> *Will lead my steps aright.*[30]

We are reminded that in all our ways we must depend on and acknowledge God.

SECURITY AND CONFIDENCE

The ancient writer reminds us that we are to trust God with all our heart. With trust the ancient writer of wisdom often links

---

30   Bryant, William Cullen. "To a Waterfowl," *Masterpieces of Religious Verse*, edited by James Dalton Morrison, (N Y: Harper & Brothers Publishers, 1948), 92.

two related nouns, according to Kenneth Aitken.[31] These twin nouns are security and confidence. When we trust God completely, we are secure people and we are confident persons. Trust in God enables us to go through life not relying on our own strength alone but living in quiet confidence on the resource of God's presence.

The Wisdom writer has assured us if we acknowledge God with all our heart, God will direct or make straight our paths. This is the promise we have from God if we love God with all our being. This promise of God assures us of the providence of God. The writer does not tell us how but God's promise of guidance is enough. How do we determine the guidance of God? Let me offer some brief suggestions.

FOLLOW THE LIGHT YOU HAVE

First, you need to follow the light that you have. I think that we sometimes do not perceive what God wants us to do more clearly because we have not followed the light God has already given us. If you are driving in your car at night, you must first move in the light that your headlights cast in front of you. As you move in that light, you are able to advance further. Some of us are not able to go any further in understanding what God wants us to do because we have been unwilling to step into the light that we already have. Michel Quoist reminds us that God expects us to live in the present moment that we have as we seek to follow God's guidance. "The only time we have control over is the present," Quoist notes. "It is now, it exists. It's not heavy to bear, and it is livable by all, on one condition: that we let the past go, and not be impatient for the future."[32]

Follow the spiritual light that you have within. This might be called spiritual intuition. It is sometimes referred to as "inner light." God is often depicted in the Bible as "light." Light is of-

---

31   Aitken, Kenneth T. *Proverbs,* (Philadelphia: The Westminster Press, 1986), 40.

32   Quoist, Michel. *With Open Heart,* translated by Colette Copeland (New York: Crossroad Publishing Co., 1986), 126.

ten used as a quality of the divine nature of God. The Gospel of John states that the logos was "the light of men" (John 1:4). Jesus is called "the light of the world" (John 8:12). His followers will "not remain in darkness" (John 12:46) but become "children of the light" (John 12:36). The writer of the First Epistle of John instructs his disciples to "walk in the light as he (Christ) is in the light" (I John 1:7). "To walk" is an idiom which means "to live." We cannot walk in darkness amid claim to have fellowship with God who is the light.

When Horace Bushnell was a teacher at Yale, the campus was experiencing a religious awakening. For some reason Bushnell could not commit his life to what was happening. He had grown up as a committed Christian but his Christian ideals had slipped away from him. He was not sure that he even believed in God anymore. He realized that he was influencing some of the students on campus who were not participating in the religious revival. He began to ask himself, "What is it that I can still believe? I believe," he said, "there is a difference between right and wrong." He felt that if God existed he would be on the side of what is right, so he decided to put his life on the side of what was right. He made the first step by acknowledging that he believed something. His belief in the difference between right and wrong was the first step that gradually began to move him back into a deeper awareness of God. Later he became one of the most noted professors and ministers in our country. He made his journey back by walking in the light that he had.

Walking daily in the light of God's presence, we are "en-lightened" in the knowledge of God's way. I believe that God sometimes works ever so slowly in the inner consciousness of our minds to guide us into deeper commitment and service for God. I am not convinced that many of us are going to receive God's will by blinding flashes of light. But I do believe that in quietness and times of prayer God sometimes speaks within our inner conscience and offers us direction and guidance.

USE YOUR REASONING ABILITY

Second, use the reasoning powers that you have. I don't know why we think that to use our mind is to go counter to what God might want us to do. Why do we think that God is always going to guide us by imparting something outside of ourselves? I heard about a man who prayed that God would guide him in making a decision and he said, "I never got any direction from God, so I just used my common sense." What makes him think that his common sense might not be the way God was guiding him? Sometimes God may be saying to us: "O.K., I have put the problem on your table. You solve it. You have got a mind. Use it." Why do we think that if we use our mind we are going against God's will? God has given us a mind so we can think. Avail yourself of that resource.

When Norman Cousins visited Albert Schweitzer in Africa, he asked him if he had a sense of direct, divine guidance that led him to Africa as a medical missionary and to give up his careers in music, theology, and philosophy. Cousins was not sure if he had asked the most obvious question or was pushing at a door he wanted to keep closed. Dr. Schweitzer looked up and said that he believed that the pursuit of the Christian ideal was a worthwhile aim for any person. After a moment, he said "that he did not want anyone to believe what he had done was the result of hearing the voice of God or anything like that. The decision he had made was a completely rational one, consistent with everything else in his own life."

"Indeed, he said, some theologians had told him that they had had direct word from God. He didn't argue. All he could say about that was that their ears were sharper than his." He said, however, that he believed in the evolution of human spirituality, and that the higher this development in the individual, the greater his awareness of God. Therefore, if by the expression, 'hearing the voice of God,' one means a pure and lively and advanced development of spirituality, then the expression was correct. This is what is meant by the "dictates of the spirit."[33] What Schweitzer was saying is that he discovered God's will and guidance for his life by using his reasoning powers. By using his mind, he was able to find God's direction for his life within.

STUDY THE BIBLE

Third, study the Scriptures. Let me send up a warning flag quickly here. Don't use the Scriptures like a Ouija board. There are some people who want to discover God's will by closing their eyes, opening their Bible, dropping their finger on a verse, and whatever that verse is, they assume that must be what God wants them to do.

I know a college student who used that method once. His finger landed on the verse, "And Judas went out and hanged himself." He decided that he must have made a mistake, so he flipped over to another passage. There his finger stopped on the verse, "Go and do likewise." This is a foolish way to use the Scriptures to determine God's guidance. I have heard of others who flip through the Bible, and when the telephone rings that signals for them to stop at whatever passage they are reading. And that will indicate what God wants them to do.

The Bible is not some book of magic that we thumb through for quick answers. When you search the Scriptures, you find the eternal principles and teachings about how God has worked in the lives of other people in the past. Then you seek to understand how you can relate these principles and teachings to your life. The Ten Commandments, the Old Testament prophets, the Beatitudes and the other teachings of Jesus, the insights of Paul and others, are all principles and guides for our lives. We don't discover God's will by finger dropping through the Bible. That approach is akin to witchcraft and magic. This is an improper use of Scripture. Saturate your life in a daily study of the Bible so its eternal truths can guide you. Seek to discern how God worked in the lives of ancient biblical persons and be open to the divine presence through prayer.

33   Cousins, Norman. *Dr. Schweitzer of Lambarene,* (New York: Harper & Brothers, 1960), 192.

WAIT WITH PATIENCE

Fourth, wait patiently for God. If there has been any lesson I have learned in life, it is that God is much more patient that I am! And that is true for all of us! God moves most of the time very slowly to accomplish God's will. On the other hand, we usually want everything right now. We want to know God's will for us in an instant. "I'm ready, God. Tell me now!" But God doesn't work that way. God waits patiently to realize the goals He intends to reach. The Scriptures advise us again and again "to wait patiently for the Lord." "Be still and know that I am God."

When I was pastor of St. Matthews Baptist Church in Louisville, Kentucky, I heard John Willingham, our youth minister, tell about his own struggle to know God's direction for his life. He told about his years of experience in a successful landscaping business in Georgia. Slowly, because of a change in economy, business got difficult. He sold his business and moved back to Knoxville to complete a degree at the University of Tennessee. Believing that God was leading him to be an agriculture missionary, he was advised to get a master's degree before he went to the mission field. After finishing his master's degree and consulting with the Foreign Mission Board, he felt that foreign missions was not what God wanted him to do. He continued to struggle to find God's guidance for his life. In the meantime, he and his wife had been working with young people in their local church. He loved that work and felt that maybe that was the area God wanted him to work. He was told that he really needed to get a seminary education if he wanted to be an effective youth minister. Again his family picked up and moved. This time to Louisville. His family became active in our church, and they began to work with our young people. Later God opened a door in our church, providing John an opportunity for service as Youth Minister.

It was fascinating to hear John and Alice tell of their pilgrimage. One door was closed. They struggled to discern God's direction for their lives. But in a slow journey, sometimes filled with delays and obstacles, they patiently discovered God's guidance. Let us remember to wait upon the Lord.

Be Nurtured by the Church

Next, draw on the resources of the Church. The spiritual heritage of those who have gone before us in the faith and some who are living today can give us guidance for discovering God's will. We can look to the Christian saints in the past and present in how they understood God's will. Their experiences might offer us guidelines for our own.

Although the Apostle Paul met Christ on the Damascus Road in a blinding flash of light, later in his life he struggled to discern God's guidance. He had wanted to preach the gospel in Spain, but he ended up in jail in Rome. He may have never understood why the door to Spain never opened for him, but his "detour" in a Roman prison was the place God used him to write letters that we are still reading today for spiritual guidance and direction.

William Cowper went through a difficult crisis in his life. He tried to commit suicide by taking drugs. He hired a carriage to drive him to the river Thames where he wanted to throw himself into the river. But something held him back, and he could not go through with it. The next day he fell on a knife blade in an attempt to stab himself, but the knife blade broke. He hanged himself, but was cut down by a friend. After all of the attempts to commit suicide had failed, he gradually passed into a rich Christian experience. Reflecting on God's providence, he later wrote a hymn:

> *God moves in a mysterious way*
> *His wonders to perform*
> *He plants his footsteps in the sea,*
> *And rides upon the storm.*[34]

---

34 Cowper, William. "Light Shining Out of Darkness," *Masterpieces of Religious Verse*, edited by Dalton, (N Y: Harper & Brothers Publishers, 1948), 10.

GOD'S WAY IS MYSTERIOUS

Finally, remember how mysteriously and unexpectedly God moves. We never know for certain how God works in the lives of people. Columbus was traveling with his son back to Italy when they stopped at a monastery outside Granada. He was discouraged and did not believe that he was going to get the resources he needed to undertake his journey across the ocean. He talked with a monk there while he was drinking water and shared his story with him. This monk introduced him to Queen Isabella who financed his trip to the new world.

Abraham Lincoln didn't know which way to turn in his life. One day he was rummaging in a rubbish barrel in Salem and found a copy of Blackstone's *Commentary on Law*. He began to read it and his life was set in a new direction.

John Calvin was traveling to Italy, but the roads were closed and he had to go through Geneva. He met Farrel there, and was invited to stay. From Geneva, his theological impact influenced much of the rest of Christendom.

Albert Schweitzer picked up a missionary journal and read about the need in Africa, and determined to become a medical missionary to Africa. God worked through that missionary journal to redirect his life.

One of the pioneers in the clinical pastoral movement in our country was Anton Boisen. In his autobiography, *Out of the Depths*, Boisen relates the story of falling in love with a woman named Alice who did not return his love. He was so crushed by this experience and an unhappy pastorate that he had a mental breakdown. While he was in a mental hospital, he was disturbed by the lack of religious help and he pioneered a movement to relate psychology and religion. He became one of the first chaplains in a psychiatric hospital and began the clinical pastoral training programs in our seminaries. The epilogue to his autobiography is entitled "The Guiding Hand." Here he states that if he had married Alice, he probably would have gone to a comfortable parish as a pastor and would never have discovered "the interrelatedness of mental disorder and religious experience" or begun the clinical training movement.[35]

God works in different ways in the lives of people. As each person is different, so may his or her guidance be varied. The affirmation from the ancient writer of wisdom is "Trust in the Lord with all your heart. Acknowledge God in all your ways and God will direct your path." I don't know exactly how God may lead your path. God may work through your reasoning ability, your inner resources, your friends, acquaintances, or by delays or obstacles. Who knows? But the one thing of which I am firmly convinced is this. God does guide our lives. When we trust God completely, we will discover God's leading. Be faithful to follow what you can clearly see in the moment. When the distant path seems dim or uncertain, take the next step you see before you. What we lack in faith or understanding dare to step forward in trust. As Dante has said, "In his will is my peace." Let us seek to know that peace. He or she who has ears to hear will hear.

---

35   Boisen, Anton. *Out of the Depths*, (New York: Harper & Brothers, 1960), 209.

CHAPTER 5

A CIRCULAR VIEW
OF LIFE

When Welton Gaddy was a former pastor in Fort Worth, Texas, he and his family attended a religious conference in another city. One night when they were sitting in the congregation, the speaker began his sermon with some rhetorical questions. That can be rather dangerous sometimes, especially when there are small children in the congregation. Gaddy's son was lying down with his head in his father's lap. The preacher began by asking: "Do you know who you are?" His small son answered in a whispered voice but loud enough to be heard. "James Welton Gaddy." "Do you know where you are from?" the preacher asked. His young son responded, "Fort Worth, Texas." "Do you know where you are going," the minister continued. "To sleep," the child said.

It is often risky to ask people, "Where are you going?" and "Where have you been?" The response of many of us is that we find ourselves going around in a circle. We seem to be coming and going from the same place where we have been and back again to where we were before. We find ourselves constantly going around and around in circles.

A group of rangers made up a part of the First, Third, and Fourth battalion in the Second World War. At one time these rangers had numbered fifteen hundred. In the battles of the Mediterranean, their forces had always been right in the heat of battle. Only one hundred ninety-nine of the fifteen hundred survived, and sixty-four received Purple Hearts. Later when they would meet each other someplace, they did not greet one another with a normal greeting like: "Hello," or "How are you?" They would ask each other instead: "How come we're still alive?" They had been surrounded by many who had died, and now they had to question why they survived when others had died.

I was in the hospital room recently with a church member when she received a phone call telling her about the death of one of her family members. A minister is often thrust into the lives of people in times of crises. During these times, one is forced to face questions about the meaning of life. Why are you still alive and what are you going to do with the life that you have? Are we going to sleep our lives away? Are we going to continue just doing what we have always done, or are we going to find some way to make our lives worth living?

The writer of the Book of Ecclesiastes does not seem to be too excited about life, does he? In many of his comments about life, he views life in a rather pessimistic way. "The sun comes up and the sun goes down," he says. "It goes full circle and comes again." (Ecclesiastes 1:5-11). "Sunrise, sunset," says the song. Life, according to the writer of Ecclesiastes, goes on and on and seems just to be circular. Greek philosophy and many of the other ancient traditions saw all of life as going around in a circle. History is circular. Whatever happened once will be repeated again. Many have viewed history in that way; it is really not going anywhere but around and around in a repetitious way.

Life Can Be Circular

Let us begin by acknowledging that a lot of life is often really circular. Much of what you and I do that is important in our lives does carry us around in certain circles again and again. Many things we do in life, like our job, family concerns, eating and sleeping cause us to walk through the same stretch of territory again and again. The repetitiousness of life doesn't mean that we have to resign from life because we move in familiar circles.

I read about a medical doctor who resigned his practice to give him more time to write. When somebody asked him why he quit medicine, he answered: "I just got tired of looking down people's throats and looking in their ears. I just got tired of it!" But who doesn't get tired? Who doesn't get tired in his or her job and weary with it, even if it is often exciting? We all get weary.

One expression which we hear constantly from young people is, "I don't want to do something; it's boring." "I don't want to go there, it's boring!" "I don't want to do that; it's boring." I hate to tell you but a lot of life is boring. We have to learn to live within the circle of boredom so we can equip ourselves to face the hard reality of living.

The Kentucky Derby has been called the most exciting two minutes in sports. Those two minutes can be exciting only because of the energy and effort which have gone into the preparation for those few minutes with several horses racing down the track toward the finish line. But the process of getting the horses ready for the race, the training of the jockeys, and all the other details can be tedious, long, and boring. The process of grooming and training a horse over and over again through the months before the Derby can be very repetitive. It looks simple and easy, but it's a circle.

DISCIPLINE AND TRAINING CAN BE CIRCULAR

It is easy to say, isn't it: "Oh, look at that famous doctor. How I wish I could be a medical doctor." But we forget the hours, days, months, and years of training and studying that he or she must endure to be a doctor. Later he has to get up at the crack of dawn, work long hours day after day after day. He has to walk in the same circle again and again. It seems glamorous to see a seminary professor all hooded up in his theological colors at graduation and say to yourself as a young student: "I want to be like that one of these days." We forget the years of training to reach a teaching post, and then all of the hours of reading book after book, preparing lecture after lecture, writing paper after paper, teaching class after class which is necessary. There is a routine which is repeated over and over again. But the same is true for lawyers, bankers, car salesmen, homemakers, and most jobs.

In the building of a new house or a church building, there are brick layers who are willing to be bored. They placed one brick after another brick on top of others. Carpenters regularly sawed, nailed, and measured and sawed, nailed and measured some more. Electricians pulled and connected wires over and over again. Construction work reveals that much of life is circular. We have to walk the same paths, go to the same job, eat meals again, go to sleep, rise up, and repeat the same process. What do we do because of that? Do we just throw our hands up and say: "It's boring and not worthwhile? I will not make the effort."

Courting can usually be exciting and enjoyable. People look forward to getting married. But we forget that married life has a tremendous amount of routineness in it. The dishes have to be washed; the house has to be cleaned; clothes need washing; meals have to be prepared; yard work needs attention; and the list goes on. Married life has a circular nature which cannot be avoided. It is usually exciting for a couple to think about having children. But someone must get up in the night with them when they are babies; feed them and care for them. Someone must change their diapers, and I have never found anybody that finds that exciting! Taking care of babies can be boring with its daily routine. But it is a circular part of life which is essential, if a baby is going to grow.

ROUTINENESS IS A PART OF LIVING

When are we going to realize that all of life is not exciting, and we cannot always live on tiptoe and in expectation. The routineness of life is a part of our living which we have to accept. The circular nature of daily living is a fact of life. Ask the teacher, farmer, truck driver, accountant, banker, dentist, realtor, and many others if this is not true?

In C. S. Lewis' *Screwtape Letters*, the senior devil is talking to some of his demons one day. They had been working a certain individual trying to draw him under the control of the forces of evil. The devil says. "Keep pressing home on him the *ordinariness* of things."[36] When we become convinced that our life is so ordinary, common, routine, and circular that it is not important and is just boring and dull, then we lose our sense of significance.

MONOTONOUS DOES NOT HAVE TO LEAD TO DESPONDENCE

We must admit that much of life is circular. But, in acknowledging that, we do not have to take the position of the writer of Ecclesiastes and give way to despair and pessimism. In the King James translation, the writers words are, "Vanity of vanity, all is vexation of spirit." The New English Bible translates this phrase: "Emptiness of emptiness." Literally the verse means vapor of vapors; it is just like thin air. There is nothing worthwhile in the world. You can't grab hold. Life isn't worth living; it just goes on and on.

What a sad concept of life. But there are many who have fallen prey to that attitude. Some of us today have that perspective. We can sit in a magnificent building like the St. Giles Cathedral in England and focus only on some negative thoughts. The beauty eludes us because of the negativity of our perspective in those moments.

Even when you are with people, your mind races to negative thoughts about them. Folks like this are constantly criticizing others and always see the worst in them. No matter how much one might try, whether his or her best efforts have been used, that is never good enough for them. They always want just a bit more. It is easy to ridicule, discourage and put others down. Too many of us have given in to this philosophy and attitude of defeatism and pessimism toward life.

Snoopy is walking along with his Beagle Scout outfit on, and he is taking some of his little bird friends on a hike. They all get lost. Charlie Brown chastises him for getting lost. "You had a compass with you. How could you get lost? Don't you realize that the

---

36   Lewis, C. S. *The Screwtape Letters* (London: Fontana Books, 1956), 14.

'N' on there stands for north?" Snoopy said, "Oh, I thought that meant nowhere."

AVOID NEGATIVITY

A lot of us have ended up nowhere in life because our view is negative. We see life only from a pessimistic viewpoint. We are not able to live our life with the sense that the circle is carrying us someplace significant.

When William Sloan Coffin was chaplain at Yale Divinity School, he used to tell the college students: "Watch it, lest fifty years from now you look back on the springtime of your lives and say 'Ah, those were the days!'— and be right." For some of us, the best time was some moment in the past. We know we are not going anywhere with our life now. We can't find any meaning, purpose, direction, or hope *now*, and that is sad.

ENLARGE YOUR CIRCLE IN LIFE

Let me also encourage you, though, as you move through the circle of life, that even in those things which you and I must do again and again, we learn to enlarge our circle. The problem for some of us is that our circle is too small. It is confined to home, or home and church, or home and the store, or home and work. We live in a very small circle. It has not grown enough to reach out and include other people and other interests. It is too narrow, too confined, and too self-contained.

A boomerang can become a proper symbol for living. The boomerang was first invented either by the Egyptians or Ethiopians. If one throws a boomerang correctly, it will always return to the one who threw it. Life is a bit like that, too. What we invest into life usually determines our dividends. You reap what you sow, the Scriptures remind us. Some of us do not reap wide returns because our focus is so narrow. We have gathered ourselves too much into ourselves, and we have not reached out and met the needs of others. Opportunities to minister in our church, community, state and beyond, are often confined to where we are in this moment. We are so self-contained that we do not reach beyond the very small circle we have lived in too long.

A young American woman married a medical doctor and they went across the world to serve in India. While there her husband contracted a strange disease, and died very suddenly. When she was sailing back home, she met a young boy on the ship whose missionary parents had also died in India. She was so distressed by her own grief that she gave no time or attention to this young boy. As the only other American on the ship and suffering from his own grief for his parents, he wanted some time and attention. But she would not respond to his need. This story took place during the Second World War. Their ship was torpedoed and everyone had to find whatever floating objects he or she could cling to until every-one could get into a life boat. The grieving widow and the grieving boy sustained each other through the weeks of their ordeal on the sea, and those who survived with them observed that it would be very difficult to say which one really saved the other - whether the woman saved the boy or the boy saved the woman. But the major point was that she finally got outside of herself and began to reach toward someone else. In doing that, her life was different.

We begin to find ourselves as we lose ourselves in doing for other people. When we reach out to help those in need, those who are hurting, in pain, or grieving, we take the spotlight off ourselves and focus on helping instead of being helped ourselves. As our circle is enlarged to include others, we begin to see life in a radically new dimension.

CHRIST IS CENTRAL TO OUR CIRCLE

Most importantly of all, those of us who live our lives daily within a circle need to have that circle intersected by the power of Jesus Christ as Lord. When He comes into the circle of our lives, He keeps life from just going round and round without meaning, but He gives it direction, plot, and hope. He gives our life character because we get outside of ourselves and into His way. The Scripture passage from John 13: 3-5 states that Jesus Christ, knowing that His origin was from God and knowing that He was going back to God, took a towel and basin and began to serve. He knew His origin and ultimate goal. We must know ours. We have come into existence out of God's creation and we are going back to God at death. Christ calls us to give our lives in full service and commitment and to quit trying to put all of our attention on what can we get out of life, but how can we be more like Christ? The question is: How can I give my life in meaning and service to help other people?

I read about a thief who had broken into an apartment. The police were puzzled for many days because they could not find any evidence to help them in discovering who it was. But then one day they found a single fingerprint on an alabaster statue of Christ on the mantle. When the thief came into the home, he evidently saw this face of Christ which seemed to be looking right at him, and before he would rob anything from the house, he reached over and turned the face of Christ to the wall so the statue would not be looking at him. They could catch him because he had left his fingerprint on the statue of Christ.

CHRIST CAN DIRECT OUR PATH

Too often, we go through life seeking to turn Christ's face away from us. We want to go our own way without another telling us which way we should go. Often we continue to move in one circle after another until we permit Christ to place His hand on us, turn us in a new direction, and point us toward life with meaning. The life He offers is enriching and fulfilling - not a life that is empty, despairing, and boring. Life in Christ is full, joyful, and radiant. This rich life is paradoxically the way of service. Our Lord girded Himself with a towel and basin, and He calls us to minister with Him. When we know that we have come from God and we are going to God, we discover that the greatest meaning in life is often found in serving. He directs our life away from defeat to victory, from despair to hope, from pessimism to joy, from ridicule to encouragement, from despondency to confidence, darkness to light. Jesus Christ gives our lives direction and keeps us from going around in meaningless circles. He leads us in the way that is going somewhere in our journey through life.

In December of 1972, *Life* magazine, which had existed for thirty-six years, came to an end. Over eighteen hundred issues had been published, and they, of course, made their last issue their swan song for the world. But it was interesting to discover, when you opened that issue to a certain place, that somehow someone had forgotten and included the card asking the readers to subscribe again. The card read: "Please start sending me Life."

There are a lot of people down in the low moments of their existence who cry out and say, "Please keep sending me 'life.'" Jesus Christ has come that you and I might have life and have it more abundantly. We must decide whether we will go in a circle which takes us away from Him in our own concerns and self-interest or whether we will follow Him and let His way guide us into a life filled with meaning and purpose. Each of us must decide which way we will go.

CHAPTER 6

THE SOUNDS
OF SILENCE

One of the popular stories circulating along hospital corridors tells of two doctors as they met in the hospital. An orthopedic surgeon is speaking with a psychiatrist and exclaims: "I don't know how you can spend all day listening to people...?" The psychiatrist responds: "Who listens?" Who indeed! Children complain that their parents never listen to them. Teachers complain that students never listen. Students complain that their teachers never listen to them. Wives complain that their husbands will not listen to them, and husbands make the same complaint. There is no question that communication, or the lack of it, is one of the biggest problems in the breakdown of marriages today.

What has happened to the one-time seemingly interested listener? He or she has disappeared and now there seems to be an eclipse of listening. The "pop prophets" from the sixties and seventies, Simon and Garfunkel, from whom I borrowed the title for this chapter, have expressed the "deaf ear" of modern life which is still unfortunately applicable today in their hit recording of "The Sounds of Silence." Note their warning as they sing about their old friend darkness, with whom they have come to talk. As they walk down narrow, cobblestone streets, they see people "talking without speaking; people hearing without listening." They continue to sing that no one dare disturb the sounds of silence as the signs on the subway walls reveal that the prophets "whisper the sounds of silence."

The sounds of silence are indeed all around us. Seldom do we really hear or listen well! In studies that have been made, it has been shown that seventy-five percent of our time is given over to communication. More than sixty percent of this time is spent in listening. This study would seem to confirm the fact that we spend more time listening than anything else. If this is true, then we certainly need to give care to the way we listen. Yet studies have shown that even when professional people listened to a lecture, and were tested immediately following it, they could recall only about fifty percent of what they had heard. Even the best among us have such poor listening habits.

Our doctors would be greatly disturbed if they were told that some of their patients retained only half of the food they ate each day. Few of us would want to send our children to college next year if we thought they were going to miss half the classes. But due to poor listening habits, college students will forget fifty percent or more of all they hear in the classrooms.

Think of the time, money, equipment, and energy that is lost every year in business and industry because of poor listening habits. If you went into a store and asked to see a dress size 12 and the clerk thought you had asked for a size 16, just look at the wasted time and energy the clerk spent in looking for something which you didn't want because she did not listen well. If I ask for a size 41 regular suit and the clerk shows me a 48 long, he and I both waste our time. How often have we received the wrong book, piece of merchandise, clothing, hat, or some other item because the person waiting on us did not listen carefully? It happens all the time, doesn't it?

One of our poets has expressed his own frustrations and we join the cry:

> *"Listen to me for a day — an hour! — a moment!*
> *lest I expire in my terrible wilderness, my*
> *lonely silence! O God, is there no one to listen?"*

Dominick Barbara's phrase, "listen for the sound of silence" has stated the difficulty of getting people to remain silent and listen. Yes, it is a paradox - the sound of silence. Only as we become silent can we hear.

AN AGE OF NOISE

Why is it so hard to hear? One of the reasons is that we live in an "age of noise." Teenagers seem never to put down their smart phones. The smart phone has almost become a part of some people's anatomy. Even on the streets we see persons with chords connected from their ears to their phones or other kind of laptops or iPads so they can listen or watch as they sit, walk or jog. Our many cell phones and televisions are loud evidence of our fear of silence. There are two kinds of people, so I'm told, those who turn on the radio or TV as they enter a room and those who turn them off. How often have you come into a room where people were engaged in conversation and felt the sting of embarrassment when everyone stopped talking and the room became quiet? Immediately someone begins to talk because we are intimidated by the quiet. We seem to feel more comfortable surrounded by noise. Silence appears threatening.

Our ability to tune out those things we do not like is mute testimony to this fact. We are masters of tuning people out. We can sit in church or in a classroom and look so engrossed in the sermon or lecture and all the time our minds are off on a wild goose chase, running after one thought or another. We may be thinking about lunch, worrying about business, making plans, or just daydreaming. Someone can be busy talking to us and we will appear to be "all ears," but while they are speaking, we are either thinking about what we will say next, or thinking about a letter unwritten or email, the job left undone at work, the washing or ironing still to be done, or that good looking new boy or girl at school.

We have learned to tune out many of the sounds of our world. We have learned to tune out the cries of affliction, pain, prejudice, hunger, and war. Their cry is drowned out by a different kind of noise. In many of our big cities, we do have to tune certain things out or we could not survive. If one lived in New York city and had the sensory ability of an African bushman, he or she soon would go mad. We do learn to shut out certain sounds, smells and sights.

A young man came to visit a friend of his who had lived all of his life beside a railroad track where trains passed at regular intervals during the day and night. After the first night in the home when he had been jarred awake suddenly by the roar of a freight train which shook the whole house and had his bed literally bouncing on the floor, the young man sat at the breakfast table the next morning, weary from a restless night, and exclaimed: "How can you sleep with those trains coming by at night?" Having lived there all his life, his host asked: "What trains?"

We learn to shut out certain sounds as a means of defense and escape. In some ways, this may be good but in some areas, it can prove extremely dangerous. Some time ago the *New Yorker* reported the story of a husband, it could be Mr. Average husband, who came home after a busy day at work and sat down in his chair in front of the TV and buried himself in the evening paper. His wife began to unload her day and her activities to him. As many husbands do, he was listening with only half an ear. After a while he decided that he had better tune in on some of it, and so he began listening just as his wife was relating that the next door neighbor had made a pass at her. Angered by what he had heard, the husband started to go next door and horsewhip his neighbor. He suddenly stopped and asked his wife when this took place? The wife replied that it had not occurred. She was only relaying a dream she had last night. Poor listening can get you into a lot of trouble sometimes.

The psalmist has directed us to "be still and know that I am God." (Psalm 46:10). In the book of Revelation one finds recorded that in Heaven there was silence for about half an hour. (Revelation 8:1). If one is talking all the time, he or she cannot listen. Hearing comes as we pause and listen. Twenty-six hundred years ago, King Zedekiah of Judah climbed the walls of the besieged city of Jerusalem and pondered the impending annihilation of his nation. The king sent for the prophet, Jeremiah, to be brought forth from his dungeon cell and inquired: "Any word from the Lord?" (Jeremiah 37:17). The question is raised again today in the midst of all the noise and uncertainty of life. Any word from the Lord? — What word would we hear?

HEAR A WORD ABOUT WORDS

An articulate person today speaks about thirty-thousand words a day. That's enough words for a good size book. By the close of our lifetime, each one of us will have spoken enough words to fill enough books to stock a good size college library. That's a lot of talk! Think of the power of words. If a word is spoken, it is carried by sound waves to the eardrum. If the word is written, it is picked up by the light waves that strike the retina of the eye and convey the message to the brain cells. Words can be powerful, sharp, incisive and penetrating or they may be dull, lifeless and abstract.

Words can create powerful images. Images play an important role in our society today. Certain images determine styles, mannerisms, tastes, and preferences. The advertising market is well aware that images and words influence what people buy, eat and wear, as well as where they go, stay, and play. We have been influenced by Beyoncé to Justin Bieber, from Brad Pitt to Mel Gibson, from "Saturday Night Live" to the Metropolitan Opera, from Richard Pryor to George Carlin, from Serena Williams to Michael Phelps, from Michael Jordan to Peyton Manning. Words sway and direct both young and old.

In Rodgers and Hammerstein's musical, *The Flower Drum Song*, a song presents brightly the question: "How will we ever communicate without communication?" How often we hear "say what you mean." But it is so difficult to communicate what we really mean. Words change their meanings so quickly. Consider the eternal word change. Can you remember when a pad was a cushion; fix was to repair; pot was something you cooked in; grass was something that grew on the lawn; a bunny was something that hopped; Beatles were something that crawled on the ground or ate rose bushes; Rolling Stones were moving rocks; thriller was a scary movie; "AC/DC" was electrical voltage; or "Facebook" was the cover on a book; or "LinkedIn" referred to an enclosed fence; or Twitter referred to "uttering a succession of small tremulous sounds" like a bird's song. Words are continuously shifting and changing because of the impact of those who use them the discovery of new technology, and how these words are interpreted in our society today.

Many, who feel that the only version of the Bible one should use is the King James Version, are unaware of the many revisions this translation has gone *through*. It was by no means static and fixed, and is vastly different today than it was in 1611. An edition in 1613 carried 300 variations, and revisions appeared in 1629, 1638 and 1762. In 1769 a revision was printed which included modernization of spelling, punctuation, etc. In the King James Version are included many words and expressions whose meanings are archaic or obsolete today. "Conversation" used to carry the meaning of "conduct" and was not a reference to speech. "Quicken" and "quick" used to mean "to give life" or "to be alive." In the 1611 version "let" and "prevent" carried a different meaning than is used today. "Let" was used in the sense of "prevent" and "prevent" was used to mean "to come before" or "precede." In one place in the Old Testament it said that "David prevented the dawning of the morning." It makes a lot of difference whether that means David stopped the sun from coming up, or, as it should be understood, he got up before the sun came up. Words and their meanings are continually changing. That is the reason the Bible must always be in constant revision. It was written originally in the language of the people and must be revised constantly to keep its meaning clear and precise.

Have you ever tried to analyze television commercials to determine what they are seeking to tell us? Consider some of the meaningless noise we have ever before us:

Razor blades that are sold to us by great tennis players who have tennis balls bopped off the head of other people on the court.

Beer that is sold by raging bulls crashing through walls. People are depicted engaging in some sport to the point of total exhaustion simply for a beer.

Recall the vision of the lonely washer repairman.

Consider the advertisements that use a "duck" to promote health insurance, or an "elephant" to sell auto insurance; or a "green lizard" to sell insurance.

The list of the absurdity of many TV commercials could be stretched endlessly. What are they trying to tell us? One message that comes through loud and clear to me is that the advertising market goes to such extremes to sell their product because they understand the public has poor listening habits. The advertising market realizes that no one can listen until you get his or her attention. The absurd is used in many commercials, it would seem, hoping that through this medium, the listener's attention can be captured.

SPEAKING WITHOUT TALKING

Words are not the only way we can express ourselves. Conversation is an intimate means of communion, but it is not the only means, nor is it the first. Persons had communion with one another before speech was developed. Even today with speech, communion can be established by a nod, a gesture, a glance, a smile, a touch, a facial motion, or a body motion. Communion can be established in a vital way without a verbal word passing.

An article entitled, "Standing Room Only For Silence," tells about the unusual performance of the French entertainer, Marcel Marceau, who can speak four languages. He does not utter a word in his performance but tells his story completely by pantomime. So successful is he with his techniques that often the audience will shout out a response to his pantomime! Have you ever witnessed the interpretation of a beautiful hymn by sign language to the deaf? The gestures are breathtaking at times, they are so suggestive and expressive, even to one who cannot understand them. Picturesque communication takes place through their signs.

Psychologists use the term "non-verbal communication" to describe the ways we express ourselves without words. In the old silent movies, Laurel and Hardy, Charlie Chaplin, and Buster Keaton were masters of this art. With a gesture, smile, nod, wink, forlorn look, or funny walk, they could spin a humorous tale. You can tell a great deal about a person by the way she bites her fingernails, squints her eyes, or the way he plays with his glasses, fingers his pen, straightens his tie or drums his fingers on the table. A kiss can be one of the most intimate means of conveying a message. Words are not important at that moment. Words are only one means of communicating. We speak with our eyes, our hands, our faces, our gestures, our touch. Every part of our body can be an expressive means of speaking without talking.

IN THE SILENCE COMES THE SOUND OF THE INCARNATE WORD

Hear again the question of King Zedekiah to Jeremiah: "Is there any word from the Lord?" Yes, the word has come, but what makes us think we will be able to hear the word? We cannot hear God's word if we do not listen. The Word of God has come, but it is not verbal. It is not just words, a smog of verbiage. Only when we pause and listen will we hear.

Jesus said the first and greatest commandment began with the call to listen: "Hear, 0 Israel." On many occasions Jesus warned His followers, "He that hath ears to hear, let him hear." The Apostle Paul directed the Church to remember that "faith cometh by hearing." Only when we listen will we be able to hear God's word. As the psalmist has reminded us, "Be still and know that I am God." When the prophet Elijah sought to find the Lord, he did not hear Him in the noise of the wind, earthquake, or the fire. He heard "a still small voice." Some have translated these words more closely to the original text as "a sound of gentle stillness." Apart from the rush, noise and hectic pace of our lives, comes "a sound of gentle stillness." The sound of God's eternal word comes to interpret the silence.

Look at poor Elijah as recorded in 1 Kings 19. He had just defeated five hundred false prophets. God had demonstrated Himself in a powerful way to Elijah on top of a mountain. Then Jezebel, that ruthless politician, begins to seek him out, and he becomes a wanted man and flees. In this scene he has fallen into the pit of despondency. He had been on the mountaintop of greatness and glory, but now he has fallen into the pit of despondency, melancholy, and defeat. He cries out wanting to know where God is, and if he, he alone, is the only faithful person still alive. He is discouraged and feels deserted. He has burned himself out. God's presence comes, but it is not in the earthquake, wind or the fire but in a sound of gentle stillness.

Now that doesn't mean that God never communicates through earthquakes. Sometimes it takes an earthquake to tumble down walls of prejudice in our lives. Sometimes houses of hate are toppled over by an earthquake of His spirit in our lives. Sometimes God comes into our life like a fire purging us, making us whole. judging us, and calling us to examine the way that we act and live. He appeared in a burning bush and a pillar of fire. So God sometimes does come as a fiery presence. And sometimes He comes as a wind blowing down the fences of old customs, traditions, clichés, and old religions and seeks to bring us the freshness of His insight.

But often God comes as a still small voice, "a sound of gentle, gentle stillness." God may speak to you through your neighbor next door who is grieving. God may speak to you through a friend who is hurting. God's sound may come to you through a teenager who is having difficulty growing up. It may come through a black hand as it reaches across the line of prejudice. It may come in a swollen stomach of a child across the sea. It may come in hungry eyes for recognition and affirmation. It may come as a quiet voice which shatters old ways and calls us to become more than we are and to see greater needs around us. It comes as the "sound of gentle stillness" calling us to respond.

Oh, we need words in religion. There is an important place for them. We can sing them. We can talk them. We can preach them. But words are not enough. There is a danger in settling for only the words of the faith. Words need to come into experience, into life and to take on flesh. When God came into the world, He didn't come *in* words - He came as "*the* Word." And the Word became flesh, and in that "enfleshment," we saw life. We saw grace. We saw glory. We saw the very power and presence and Spirit of God working in our world. (See John 1:1-14). In Jesus Christ, God has made His word known to us, and in that life of lives we saw what life could be. Through that Word, your life and my life are touched and we are enabled to have words to live by, to speak or preach by, and to think by.

The earthquake, the fire and the wind are only the fringe of His garment, only the shadow of His presence. God comes as a sound of gentle stillness seeking to communicate to you and to me. The sound that comes to interpret the silence is not found in the noise of words, written or verbal, but is heard in the Living Word. "In the beginning was the Word, and the Word was with God, and the Word was God .... And the Word became flesh and dwelt among us, full of grace and truth; we have beheld his glory, glory as of the only Son from the Father." (John 1:1,14)

Perry Biddle, a minister friend I knew, had gone to Greenock, Scotland and was preaching one Sunday in a Congregational Church. He preached on the text that day, "The Lord God Omnipotent Reigneth." He used that text several times in his sermon, and then when he got toward the end of his sermon, in almost a shout. He said, "The Lord God Omnipotent Reigneth." As he was standing at the door greeting the people as they left, an official of the church told him about two ladies as they approached. "These two ladies, he whispered, "are almost completely deaf." As Biddle greeted one of the elderly ladies she said to him: "'I didna hear anything you said today, Minister, except 'The Lord God Omnipotent Reigneth!'" "But," she continued, "that's all that really matters, isn't it?" The Lord reigns in our life, and God seeks to come sometimes through the earthquake, sometimes through the wind, and sometimes through the fire. But often God comes as a sound of gentle stillness. "He that has ears to hear, let him or her hear."

CHAPTER 7

HAVING A FAITH THAT MATTERS

Several years ago I had the privilege of serving as pastor of a church that was located two blocks from one of the state universities in Virginia. Several hundred college students would often attend our worship services. These students pushed my mind and creativity to make the faith understandable for them or to get them even to consider it. One day a knock came on my study door. On opening the door, I discovered a young college woman standing there. She asked if she could talk with me for a few moments. She came in, and we began to chat. In her story she informed me that she had grown up in a home where her parents never went to church. She had never gone to church before in her life until she came to college. She had started attending our church with a friend. The more she came, and the longer she listened, she soon realized that there was something missing in her life. "You have talked about faith," she said. "I would like to have faith, but I really do not understand what it is or how I can get it. Can you tell me?"

She is joined by many others who want to understand what faith is and how they can get it. Faith is a word that those of us in religious circles throw around so easily. But I sometimes wonder how much we understand faith or really have it. The ancient psalmist in Psalm 73 knew the struggle and longed to have a meaningful faith.

THE PSALMIST'S FAITH WAVERS

The writer of Psalm 73 was a man whose faith had begun to waver. In fact, he indicates that it had almost slipped away. He looks out on life and doesn't understand what he sees. He had been faithful in his worship of God. He had been upright, righteous, loyal and yet he had experienced difficulties and disappointments. Evidently, he had suffered some personal pain, or financial losses, or some kind of near disaster. It is not possible to determine what his tragedy may have been. During this struggle, his faith almost crumbled. He looked at the prosperity of the wicked around him and exclaimed: "God, I don't understand it. I have been faithful and chaste. But, look at the wicked folks. They never give you a nod. They even thumb their nose at you and say, 'How does God know what I do?' Yet they continue to prosper. They do not seem to have problems and illness like I do. I don't understand it, God." His faith was reeling and he wasn't sure about life, religion, or God. The psalmist wondered if his faith was useless. "I thought that if I had faith strong enough I would not have difficulties or suffering, and I would prosper. But I have had faith, and I have not prospered, and my burdens have been heavy."

IS FAITH USELESS?

Does that mean that faith is really useless? There are a lot of folks who have come to that conclusion. Communism forcefully asserts that "religion is the opiate of the people." Religion, according to this philosophy, puts persons to sleep so they do not face reality. I read a play once where one of the characters declares that "religion is a chloroform mask into which the weak and unhappy stick their face to escape life." We have to admit that there are some who regard religion as an infantile way of meeting life's struggles. These persons believe that religion is only for weak persons, who are unable to face the difficulties of life with their own strength and stamina. The psalmist seemed to be questioning whether or not his personal anxieties were pulling him in this direction.

The psalmist's personal problem had pushed him to wrestle with the question of why good people suffer. As he looked at the prosperity of the wicked and his own tragedy, he was gripped with doubt and envy. His difficulties pushed him to think through his religion and its impact on his life. He asked himself, "How can I believe in God in the light of everything that is happening to me and in the world? Life doesn't seem to make any sense." Confusion arose in his mind. "It is painful for me to think about the unfairness of evildoers, selfishly getting wealthy and my own peril," he noted. "It gives me a headache when I try to understand the inequities of life and what place religion is supposed to have. I can't put it all together."

He had stopped going to worship, felt his spirit grow bitter, and was on the verge of apostasy. Why good people suffer and the wicked sometimes prosper are issues which godly persons struggle with in every age. Any thinking person will raise them.

SOME TRY TO IGNORE DIFFICULT QUESTIONS

How do some religious folks answer these questions? They have a simple solution! Many quit thinking! They decide that it is far easier not to think about these problems. If you ignore them, they might go away. They caution you not to think about such matters. They might disturb your faith. How many times have you heard someone give this advice: "Oh, don't think about questions like that. It might shake your faith." What kind of faith do you have if it can be shaken by questions raised by science, philosophy, or everyday sufferings? Faith should be able to withstand whatever questions or issues we meet in every walk of life. Robin Meyers, pastor of the Mayflower Congregational Church in Oklahoma City, boldly asserts, with which I strongly agree, that "Christianity requires no sacrifice of the intellect; it can withstand any question we dare to ask and any answer we are brave enough, in the service of truth, to offer."[37]

SOME EQUATE FAITH WITH CREDULITY

Unfortunately, some of us have given up thinking and assumed that faith is credulity. This approach is seen in a conversation be-

---

37   Meyers, Robin. *Saving Jesus from the Church* (New York: HarperOne, 2009), 218.

tween Alice and the White Queen in *Through the Looking Glass*. The White Queen claims that she is one hundred-and-one years, five months and one day old. "I can't believe that," says Alice. "Can't you?" observes the Queen. "Try again. Draw a long breath and shut your eyes." Is that what faith is? Take a deep breath, close your eyes, and then accept something blindly. Don't think! Just believe. Do you remember what Jesus said was the first and the greatest commandment? "You shall love the Lord your God with all your heart, and with all your soul and with all your strength, and with all your *mind*!" (Matthew 22:37). We are not to give up thinking through a problem even when it is painful or unpleasant. We have a sacred responsibility to use our mind.

MANY FEEL INSECURE

The doubts and envy through which the psalmist had gone had shaken his confidence and left him feeling insecure. He saw the wicked folks prospering, enjoying good health, and living in luxury while his family suffered with poverty, illness, and difficulties. He wondered if God was asleep or if God cared. He questioned whether his faith did any good at all. His insecurity led him to the edge of abandoning his belief in God. He wanted his religion to give him solid base for life. But his foundation seemed to be crumbling. His feet were slipping under him. He felt they had been cut out from under him. He wanted to feel secure and on solid ground. But he no longer felt secure.

One of my favorite philosophers, Charles Schulz, has an interesting theological tome entitled *Security is a Thumb and a Blanket*. In this small book, Schulz gives several pictures of security.

"Security," he says, "is having someone to lean on."

"Security is carrying an extra safety pin in your purse."

"Security is owning your own home."

"Security is having someone listen to you."

"Security is knowing all your lines" (in the school play).

"Security is (sitting in school and) knowing you won't be called on to recite."

"Security is hearing your mother in the kitchen when you come home from school."

"Security is being able to touch bottom when you're in the swimming pool."

"Security is having the music in front of you."

"Security is having a big brother."

"Security is knowing you're not alone."[38]

We all grope for some kind of security in life. We want to have a good job, a happy family, excellent health, enough money to live well, and face life free of problems. But religion has never promised us this. The Scriptures give us the assurance that no matter what happens to us, whether it is tribulation, distress, persecution, suffering, pain, or whatever, it cannot separate us from God. (Romans 8:38-39). Nothing can separate us from God and that is a different kind of security than the world often offers.

A SENSE OF THE PRESENCE OF GOD

The psalmist, like many of us, had put his faith in a narrow understanding of religion, and when that seemed to be shaken, his religious base seemed to crumble under the strain. Seeking an answer to his struggle, the psalmist entered his place of worship. In the sanctuary before God, he finds an answer to his dilemma. But he does not get a simple answer to all of his questions about why good people suffer or why the wicked prosper. But in the midst of his worship, he has a sense of the presence of God. The presence of God is so strong and real to him that he suddenly realizes that he does not have to find answers to all his questions. While he is in the sanctuary, his mind is filled with thoughts of former days when he has experienced God. An inner sense of peace and joy overpowers him. In the presence of God, he finds security and peace. What he

---

38 Schulz, Charles M. *Security is a Thumb and a Blanket* (San Francisco: Determined Productions, 1963).

discovered in the sanctuary was that religion is the ground of his whole being. He must live by faith.

ALL LIFE IS GROUNDED ON FAITH

The psalmist is right. All of life is built on faith. You don't think so? Then reflect on it for a moment. Did you ever consider how much of our daily living is dependent on faith? We put our trust in the alarm clock to awaken us each morning. We put our lives in the hands of others as we eat the food contained in packages, cans, and frozen containers. When we ride on a bus, train, or plane, we commit our lives to the safety of the driver, the engineer, or the pilot. We trust our doctors, dentists, and druggists with our lives and health almost daily. In case of trouble we depend on our policemen and lawyers to protect us. We put our money in the bank in faith that it will be there when we want it. The letter you wrote last night has been entrusted to the post office for safe delivery.

We entrust our minds to our teachers and professors, confident that they will give us sound instruction. Every marriage is built on trust and fidelity, and children trust parents to meet their needs. You sat down in a chair in confidence that it would support you. We put our trust daily, hourly, and even every minute in people, gadgets, machines, maps, books, and countless other things. Sometimes persons, things, and institutions fail. But we still have to go on living by having faith in persons and things. If not, then life simply disintegrates. Faith is essential.

Our lives are lived each day in mutual trust and confidence. We are able to trust because we are aware of a deeper faithfulness that is the ground of all confidence. The faithfulness of God is the basis of the stability of the universe outside of us, within us, and between men and women.

A group of men had been sitting around a table engaged in conversation. One of the men had become very violent. Finally, he jumped up in a rage and stormed away from the table, opened a door, walked through it, and slammed it behind him. Another man, who was sitting at the table said, "Thank goodness he has gone." The owner of the house said, "No he hasn't. That was a closet."

Many people try to reject faith and say they don't need religion. When they do, they often discover that they have exited into a closet! Without faith, life comes to a dead end. Life is built on faith in other persons, institutions, things, and ultimately in God. It is the ground of our being.

HOW DOES FAITH BEGIN?

How does faith begin? It may begin, Jesus said, in a small way like a tiny mustard seed that is planted in the ground. Like a tiny seed, faith may have a small beginning. Faith may be like a tiny piece of yeast that you put in dough to make it rise. From that small beginning, a process of growth takes place.

You and I can remember many persons who planted seeds that began our faith process. I remember seeds planted by my parents, grandparents, and teachers I had in Sunday School whose names I can no longer recall but I can still see their faces. Many persons across the years of my life have planted seeds to begin, nourish, and cultivate my faith process.

AN UNCLEAN IMAGE

Jesus used the figure of leaven (Luke 13:21), which was considered by the scribes and Pharisees as unclean. Could it be that Jesus used an image that was considered unclean because it was symbolic of His disciples- tax collectors and uneducated fishermen - whom many thought were unclean? From this small beginning - a group of twelve, eleven after one betrayed Him, and not more than five hundred after the resurrection - was the beginning of the Church.

Our faith may begin small, but the mystery of life is seen in a tiny seed growing into a tree. Our faith may begin in a small way but from that small start, it does not remain static but is growing and developing.

MANY PERSONS NURTURE OUR FAITH

Do you remember the persons who have nurtured your faith? Some persons who touched my life are vivid to me. Several years ago I traveled to Raleigh, North Carolina to attend a banquet in honor of one of the professors I had at Southeastern Seminary, Dr. Stewart Newman. Dr. Newman was eighty years old then. He has taught thousands of students through the years. He had the most profound effect on my thinking of any teacher I had in seminary. I made that long trip so I could be present at the banquet to express my appreciation for his influence on me.

FAITH IS A GROWING PROCESS

Many stories were told at the banquet about the way students tried to model Dr. Newman. Dr. Newman always had very chapped lips and used to rub a ChapStick balm on his lips to keep them from cracking. It was one of his trademarks. He would lecture for a while, pause and rub some of the ChapStick on his lips. It was always interesting to observe rising young "theologs," with their small ChapStick containers in hand, talking about religion and life, and pausing in their discussion to rub some ChapStick on their lips. He left his mark in many ways on the lives of students. Many have left their mark on us.

In the parable in Matthew 13:31-33, Jesus notes that once the mustard seed has been planted then it grows into a tree where birds nest in its branches. Faith is not only to have a beginning point, but it is to continue growing. The image which Jesus used to describe the beginning point of faith was new birth - a birth from above. After the initial birth of faith, your faith should expand and continue to grow. If you are no taller now as a Christian than you were when you first began, you really haven't understood faith. Faith *is* a growing process. It is not merely a one-time experience. As Paul writes in one of his epistles, "I have been saved; I am being saved; and I will be saved." Our salvation has a point of beginning but it is also a process of becoming. We are always challenged to move forward.

Yeast is a disturbing force in dough and causes it to rise. In the same way, Jesus is constantly a disturbing force in our lives, challenging us to grow. A small girl had gone away from home for the first time to visit some friends. That night, when it was time for bedtime, she began to cry. The mother of her friend came over and put her arm around her and asked: "Alice, are you homesick?" She said, "No, I'm not homesick. I'm here sick!"

FAITH IS A CONTINUOUS COMMITMENT

Michel Quoist, a priest of Le Havre, France, observes how difficult it is for people to make lifelong commitments. "Faithfulness is then one's ability to stick with his choice," he notes, "the will to fight for it, and turn away any obstacles into positive elements on his chosen path." "Unfaithfulness is a disease afflicting both individual and society," he continues. "Society throws the individual into new experiences which are never brought to any conclusion. Unfaithfulness is to be put off by any obstacles; weakness is man's downfall. Constantly uprooted, he can never reach maturity and bear fruit."[39] Choosing to be faithful on the journey through life is never easy.

Jesus Christ comes into our lives again and again to make us "here sick." He does not want us to be satisfied with where we are in our spiritual pilgrimage. Christ continuously challenges us to be open to Him so that His spirit can penetrate our lives and lead us further along in our spiritual pilgrimage. If we confirm that Christ is alive and still present among us, where can we be sure to find Him? Sometimes His presence is revealed in the needs of a person who crosses our path today; or in the supportive embraced of a friend in our own moment of need; or when we share a meal with a friend; or when we visit someone in jail, the hospital, or a nursing home; or in the witness of a new-born Christian; or when you see

39 Quoist, Michel. *With Open Heart*, translated by Colette Copeland (New York: Crossroad Publishing Co., 1986), 117.

someone take a difficult stand for justice; or see a brother or sister lift up someone who has fallen into depression or hopelessness; or when we gather in worship at the Lord's Table; or in endless other times and appearances. Christ crosses our path in unknown times and ways and summons us to follow.

Christ is continuously beckoning us to see and hear him in the multitude of faces and needs that rise up to meet us in our daily pilgrimage. He wants us to grow and become more like our heavenly Father. Faith is not a way of thinking that gives us the answers to all of our questions. Faith does not offer the answers in the back of the book of life. Faith is a commitment - a trust. To use Kierkegaard's image, faith is a leap into the unknown. The leap of faith is like jumping into water where you can't touch bottom. Real faith puts you in absolute dependence on God. Faith is a commitment of trust where you realize that unless you can trust God who has created life, your life will only float without direction. Without Christ, life seems futile and without meaning. Like the mustard seed, faith may begin small, but it should keep on growing throughout our lives.

Several years ago, I read how a suspended bridge was built across the Niagara River. This bridge was constructed years ago before we had the modern equipment we have today. The construction crew began by floating a kite across the river with a tiny thread attached to it. Someone on the other side of the river caught the kite and the thread. Next they tied a piece of string to the thread, and then pulled the string across the river. Then they tied a piece of rope to the string and pulled the rope across. Finally they tied a cable to the rope and pulled the cable across. Only then were they able to begin the construction of the bridge. The work began with a thread. Our faith may begin in a small way, but hopefully it will grow. If we have a faith that really matters, we will be open, growing, and developing. We know that we have never arrived spiritually. We have all eternity to grow. Let us begin.

CHAPTER 8

HEARING THE CALL
TO BE MORAL IN AN
IMMORAL WORLD

"Who would know?" the young woman asked herself, "My husband is off in the service and I am lonely. My boss has been good to me. He has invited me to go with him to his cottage in the mountains for the weekend. No one else would ever know. Why not?" She struggles with the kind of issue that many often face. She is confronted with the whole question of moral decisions. For some, life is viewed mostly in shades of gray. For others, it seems to be painted in very black colors. We can pick up the morning paper and read of bank robberies, or where someone ran off with the company funds, or where some industries are being sued due to chemicals that they have dumped into our waters, or where drug companies are being sued due to false claims which they have made for their products, We read where a man has raped and killed dozens of women and has no sense of remorse; or where a young teenager on drugs kills some of his best friends or where some students shoot other students and teachers. We read where people are willing to lie and cheat their way in business and prepare their income tax forms without scruples, and strive to get by any way they can whether it is legal or not.

WE MAKE MORAL DECISIONS EVERY DAY

There are some who have turned white lies into black lies and every shade in between, because morality has nothing much to do with reality for them. Moral decisions face us on every corner. What are we to do? A football team may have already been given their orders by the coach on what they should do to get the place kicker into the game with just a few seconds left and no time outs remaining. At the appropriate time the coach's plan is put into action and the right guard rolls over pretending that he has something wrong with his leg. When the officials stop the game, and come over to give assistance to him, it gives the coach time to get the place kicker onto the field. Later one notices as the ball goes through the uprights that the young man whose leg seemed to be in such pain a few moments before is now seen leading the cheers and jumping up and down.

A mother is in the grocery store doing her weekly shopping and her young child takes a package of cookies off the shelf and eats a portion of them while the mother is in another part of the store. When the mother returns and notices that her daughter has consumed half the package, she folds it up and puts it back on the counter and then, goes through the line and pays for her groceries. Several persons who witnessed what the child has done call it to the attention of the clerk. But the mother denies it. Contrast that with the father who brings his child back to the store to teach him a lesson because he had taken a candy bar and not paid for it.

Moral questions also meet us in school. A young high school student realizes that she does not know the answers to the geometry test, and sitting right in front of her is the brain of the class and his paper is uncovered. All she has to do is look and she can see the answers. Note another example: a television executive announces that what we need on television is more violence and more bosoms. Many of our contemporary films exploit sex and violence, linking them together in the minds of the viewers, and planting seeds in the heads of our young people that violence and sex go together. Is it any wonder that society is distorted by these movies?

Moral struggles do not always happen in a faraway world. One of the most disarming disclosures that came to me while I was teaching in one of our seminaries several years ago was the sign in the seminary bookstore that read: "Please stop stealing the Bibles." A student was also caught going out of the campus bookstore stealing a book on Christian Ethics. The seminary later installed a monitoring system as students leave the library because of the many books that have been stolen. What does this indicate about our ethical breakdown even among some "rising" ministers? What has happened to the morals in our world when even ministerial students do not have morals? "Theism is not a prerequisite to being moral," Paul Simmons writes. "Christians relate their moral witness to faith commitments, which provide strong incentives and guidance for ethical wisdom and behavior. But they have no monopoly on morality. At times Christians come off looking rather shabby when compared to certain humanists of high ethical or moral character."[40] That is certainly a strong reminder to us of the moral challenge before us.

TONES OF GRAY

For many, moral values seem to be painted not in clear colors but in tones of gray. There is nothing that appears in black or white anymore. It all appears multicolored, and you and I are told to take our choice and pick whatever color we may want. We are told to live on the raw edge. After all, you only go around once. You **are** only young once. Forget caution; don't be old fashioned. This is your day; express yourself. Take your last fling; enjoy yourself. Eat, drink, and be merry. We are living in **a day** and age in which the moral standards are not lifted very high for all persons. Our moral values have slipped, and too often we **are** mirrors of the society around us. In a recent Gallop Poll, more than 80 per cent of people in the United States said that moral values were only fair or poor and will continue to get worse.[41]

A young bride was fixing her first ham. She cut off both ends of the ham before she placed it in the oven. Her husband asked, "Why do you cut off both ends of the ham?"

---

40 Simmons, Paul D, editor, *Freedom of Conscience* (Amherst, New York: Prometheus Books, 2000), 12.

41 "U. S. Moral Values Ratings at Lowest Point in 7 Years," *The Richmond Times Dispatch*, May 26, 2017. A 6.

"Well, my mother has always done that," she replied, "and I'm just doing what she did."

The next time the couple was over at the mother-in-law's house the son-in-law asked her: "Why do you cut off both ends of the ham before you put it in the oven?"

"Well, it's the only way I can get the ham to fit in the size pan I have," she responded.

Too many people in the world today are trying to cut off both ends of issues to make them fit into pans of conformity that are too small for them. Others have taken the values of our society and cut the ends off them and reduced their standards to the level of doing what they want any place, anywhere. These people live by the rule, "If it makes you feel good, do it. " "If it feels OK to me," they say, "is that really hurting anybody else?"

TEST YOUR VALUES

Paul faced this kind of problem in the Corinthian church. (See 1 Corinthians 6:9-20). He was writing to a people who were claiming to be Christians with very corrupt moral standards. He challenged them to be moral in a very immoral society. He asked them first to test their slogan, "Everything is lawful." "Test that slogan," he said, "to see whether it is true," "I am free to do anything." "Yes," he says, "that is true to an extent. We are free to do anything, but everything you may do, may not be helpful for you. It may not be helpful to others, and using your freedom with absolute license, may in turn cause harm to you and to others in society." (1 Corinthians 9 & 10)

Then, Paul began some of his pointed statements: "do you not know." He asked them, "Do you not know that when you link your life with a prostitute you distort your own body because you engage in corrupt behavior." Some of the Corinthians thought that it did not make any difference what one did with his body because one day the body would die, and only the spirit would live on. They thought that anything you wanted to do with one's body was OK.

The body was not a real concern but only one's motive or intent was the real issue involved. Paul declared that this was not true. When your body is linked with prostitution it, too, becomes corrupted. He asked: "Do you not know that you are the temple of God? Do you not know that you are supposed to glorify God in your body?" "Yes," he says, "you have freedom, but you don't have freedom to do just anything you may want to because you must see how you use your freedom in relationship to God and to other people." When you treat other people as less than persons, then, not only have you distorted yourself but you have distorted them.

I read once about a judge in Kentucky who used a certain test for sanity. This test was a simple one. A person was brought into a room and a bucket of water was placed in front of him with a spigot above it turned on with the water running into the bucket. The man would be asked to empty the bucket of water with a dipper. If the man tried to empty the bucket of water without turning off the spigot, the judge knew that the man was not sane.

Absolute Freedom is a Myth

Part of our problem in society is that we are trying to correct our moral problems without getting back to the source and turning them off. A part of the origin of our problem in morality is the belief in absolute freedom. Absolute freedom is a myth because no one can do anything that he or she may want to do at any moment without regard for other people. My actions and your actions involve others, and we are never totally isolated in what we say or do in any particular moment. Michel Quoist states that truth this way:

> True freedom doesn't mean being able to do anything you please with your body, heart and soul, when you wish, with no restraints or taboos. This sort of freedom only betrays an absence of freedom. It's a form of total alienation; man giving in, on his knees, to all compulsions. It's going backwards, reverting to his animal condition. An animal lives by its instincts,

programmed to fulfill its needs and its growth. But man must master his life and gradually learn how to direct it.[42]

RULES HAVE THEIR PLACE

Rules do have importance in life. Persons are, of course, more important than rules. Jesus indicated that persons were more important than regulations about the Sabbath Day. Persons were more important than the rigid legalism of the Jewish system that focused on minor details of the law. But Jesus did give us some principles about life in the Sermon on the Mount and in His other teachings. His teachings offer guidance on how we are to think about ourselves and how to relate to others in society. To say that there are no rules by which a Christian lives and that each is free to make up his or her own rules is to misrepresent the Christian faith. The Ten Commandments are still valid as basic guidelines for living. To follow Christ effectively we seek to incorporate the principles of His life and teachings into our own life.

A father of twelve children who lived in a house with only one bathroom, once said: "Rules are not an option here. They are a necessity!" And so are moral principles. But if rules and laws go against the moral principles we have learned from the teachings of Jesus, they need to be challenged. "When laws are unjust and do not conform to the gospel," Libby Grammer writes, "Christians have the responsibility to address them from a faith-based perspective, just as Jesus did in first century Palestine."[43] In the reality of false "laws" like slavery, segregation, some immigration policies, the lack of equal job opportunities and equal pay for all sexes, bad environmental laws that destitute our planet and others, the Christian is obligated to stand for justice and moral rightness.

---

42 Quoist, Michel. *With Open Heart*, translated by Colette Copeland ((New York: Crossroad Publishing Co., 1986), 128.

43 Grammer, Libby Mae. *Privilege, Risk, and Solidarity: Understanding Undocumented Immigration through Feminist Christian Ethics* (Eugene, Oregon: WIPF & STOCK, 2017), 46.

MORALITY IS NOT JUST PRIVATE
BUT NEEDS TO TOUCH ALL OF SOCIETY

When we try to live in the world, rules are not just optional, they are essential. This is true not only in individual relationships but most especially when we move to the wider dimension of society at large. What I do privately not only affects me, but it also touches other people. In society, I may live a private moral life but my morality must also move over into the business world where I work, and in the industrial and financial world in which I am involved. "He who claims he doesn't need anyone is either ignorant or a liar," Michel Quoist writes, "because he lives thanks to other people who have engendered life since the beginning of time. If he refuses to live for others, he is a parasite. He grows by feeding off his brothers."[44]

Over eighty years ago Reinhold Niebuhr, one of the great moral theologians of the last century, wrote a book entitled *Moral Man and Immoral Society*. In this book, he addressed the issue of morality in one's private life and the difference in morality in our business, industrial, national and other collective areas. Persons can often do very immoral things in the collective areas of life and never see how that is immoral. Niebuhr's challenge echoes the biblical demand that morality is an absolute necessity in our business practice and in all our public as well as private relations with people. Morality is not limited to one's private life, as important as that is, but moral values should permeate our relationships in business, industry, government, and other collective institutions. Walter Rauschenbusch has reminded us that "sin is not a private transaction between the sinner and God." "Humanity always crowds the audience-room when God holds court," he declares.[45] Amos had cried for justice in the land of Israel, "seek good and not evil ... Hate evil and love good; enthrone justice in the courts" (Amos 5:14-15, NEB).

---

44 Quoist, Michel. *With Open Heart,* 42.
45 Rauschenbusch, Walter. *A Theology for the Social Gospel* (New York: The Macmillan Co., 1917), 48.

MORALITY IS GROUNDED IN GOD

Notice, secondly that Paul also says that our morality is linked with God. We are "God's temple." "Glorify God with your body." Our morality is directly related to God. Morality is not merely what one thinks is correct in the moment. Too many people depend on their conscience alone. They assume that if one thinks it is the decent thing to do that will make it okay. They declare that they will let conscience be the guide. I am sometimes very troubled by some people who want to follow their conscience, because their conscience does not seem strong enough morally to give them the kind of guidance which they need for a valid decision.

In John Galsworthy's novel, *Maid in Waiting*, there is a scene in which Dinny is talking with her mother about God and daily living.

> "Providence is a wash-out, Mother" Dinny said. "It's too remote, I suppose there is an eternal Plan but we're like gnats for all the care it has for us as individuals." "Don't encourage such feelings, Dinny; they affect one's character."
>
> "I don't see the connection between beliefs and character. I'm not going to behave any worse because I cease to believe in Providence or an after life ... No: I'm going to behave better; if I'm decent it's because decency's the decent thing; and not because I'm going to get anything by it."
>
> "But why is decency the decent thing, Dinny, if there's no God?"[46]

OUR CONSCIENCE MAY NOT BE THE BEST GUIDE

And that is the question, isn't it? When we push decency back far enough and remove it from any relationship to spirituality and God, we begin to see shades of gray and black creeping in when morality is determined by every passing fad and contem-

---

46   Galsworthy, John. *Maid in Waiting* (New York: Charles Scribner's Sons), Chapter XXVI

porary notion. Many views of decency are based merely on social customs of right and wrong without relating them to God at all. The present generation, that is seeking to live a decent life, is still a product of a life which may have been influenced by parents who believed in God and the moral goodness that has been revealed in Christ. Now that person may have drifted away from God and the church, so what "rootage" for their morality will they pass on to their children? When decency has no spiritual roots, it is based primarily on what an individual thinks is right or wrong. I am very frightened of those who want to let their conscience be their primary guide. Some people have too easily and quickly let their conscience become twisted and distorted by all kinds of negative influences upon it.

During the Second World War, while being trained at Kelly Field, young pilots were told by their instructors that they had to learn to trust their instruments implicitly or they would be killed. One day a pilot was flying in a storm and he kept feeling like his plane's right wing was too low. He continued to pull it up more and more until he felt his straps pressing tightly against his body. He couldn't understand why they were so tight. He wanted to loosen them when he got a moment. Then suddenly he thought, "I had better look at my instruments." When he did, he was flying upside down in the wrong direction. The words came home to him from his instructor: "Fly by your instrument board. Trust it and not your feelings."

Too many people simply rely on their own feelings about what is right and they have not grounded themselves in a vital relationship to Jesus Christ as Lord who gives direction on how to live life. We go off on our own without clear direction or certain standards. It should not be just one's opinion, but we look to Christ as the model and guide for ethical behavior.

A Christian's Walk Will Be Different

In the third place, when my life is related to God, then I am going to live differently because of that connection. As Paul said, "You are not your own. You are bought with a price." (1 Corinthians 6:20) Part of his reference here was to the fact that the people in this early Corinthian church, lived in a city where temples had been built to love goddesses. The prostitutes of this love goddess would often walk the streets, and solicit trade, and some of the Christians would buy the prostitute and engage in sex with her. Paul condemned this act and warned them that they had identified themselves with prostitutes and had become one with them. That union was wrong, Paul believed, because that unity was reserved for the sexual relationship within marriage. Otherwise in the eyes of God, it is sin. There is no such thing as casual sex.

There is no such thing as sex with a prostitute that is not immoral. This relationship distorts and twists one's life. You cannot say I can be sexually involved with somebody else other than my mate and it doesn't make any difference, because it does. There is no such thing as *just* a physical relationship. Paul knew that our physical relationship affects our spiritual life. Casual sex corrupts, and destroys one's spiritual life.

You Are Bought with A Price

Paul said, "You are bought with a price." Often when we hear that phrase we think that Paul is writing about the ransom which Christ gave for us. But John Ruef, a New Testament scholar, believes that the real reference here is still to prostitution. Just as one would buy a prostitute and use her as he wanted to, so one had been bought by God and now belonged to God. Through this crass analogy Paul calls the Christians to glorify God in their bodies. Ruef acknowledges that this might not be "a very delicate way of putting it but the Corinthians (to whom Paul was writing) were probably not very delicate people."[47] Paul's words strike with force and clarity. "Live your life without being related in this corrupt way to prostitutes so that you can walk in purity with Christ." Paul calls them to remember that they do not have a body, but they *are* a body. Spirit and body are intertwined.

I have often wondered if we would do certain things, if we would give it the publicity test. How would you like for certain acts or deeds which you have done to be reported in the local newspaper, or on the local television, or Facebook or to be reported in the paper of your church or in the community? None of us may want some dark deeds done in the shadows to be put into the public eye. But one of the tests for our morality might be, "Can it stand the test of daylight and exposure in the public arena? Can it stand the public test of those around me — my friends, and others? Do I want private acts to be known in public circles? "You won't even achieve enduring external success," David Brooks attests, "unless you build a solid moral code."[48]

Some politicians have later gotten into great difficulty because of indiscrete acts they engaged in earlier in life. So, you and I should seek to live in such a way that our lives are not destroyed later by the acts we may do in the darkness or in times of weakness. Learn to let the test of publicity remind us that our moral lives are evidence that we have been bought with a price and that we are seeking to glorify God in our bodies.

LIVE ON A HIGHER PLANE

Paul says, fourth, if we have committed our lives to Christ, and if we are seeking to let our bodies be God's holy temple, then we are called to live on a higher plane in the world. We shall not live like those who are without Christ. We shall live as moral people in an immoral society. We do not live like the crowd but Christ is

47 Galsworthy, John. *Maid in Waiting* (New York: Charles Scribner's Sons), Chapter XXVI.

48 Brooks, David. *The Road to Character* (New York: Random House, 2015), 12.

our model and guide. We follow the narrow way and march to a different drummer. We follow the one who lifts a higher standard. We shall seek to be His light and salt in the world, so that people can see by our walk with Christ that we are radically different.

I read several years ago about how a small animal, the ermine, is captured in the wintertime. This small creature's fur in the summertime is brown all over except for a white spot on its tail, but in the wintertime, its fur becomes snow white. When hunters want to capture this animal, they simply force it toward the mud pits. When the animal with its beautiful white fur would get close to the mud pit, it would yield up its life rather than soil its fur.

I wonder if we have understood the high moral demands of Christ. "Glorify God in your body." "You are *God's* temple." Will we stop before the forces of evil and corruption because we do not want to be spotted and tainted by them? We are challenged to stand in the courageous tradition with Moses before Pharaoh, with Jesus before Pilot, with Paul before King Agrippa, with Luther before the Roman Bishops, with John Bunyan before the English courts, with Martin Niemoller before Hitler, and with Martin Luther King, Jr. before the white establishment. These persons stood up for their convictions — at great personal cost. They were not corrupted as they let right prevail.

A Christian should not be willing to say, "I will go along with what everybody else does." As a Christian, there are values in your life for which you will stand and not be persuaded to move away from them. We need people with this kind of integrity in business, in government, and in every walk of life. We need people in public places whose integrity is without question, and their word is their bond, and who can be trusted and relied upon to do what they promise.

A very moving play for me is the one by Thomas Bolt entitled *A Man for All Seasons.* In this play Sir Thomas More was appointed Archbishop of Canterbury. Henry VIII had married Catherine, a princess of Spain, and ascended the English throne as king. Later he grew tired of her and wanted to divorce her because she could not bear him children. He requested that the Archbishop approve his marriage of Anne Boleyn, after he had rejected Catherine. More refused to do this because it required him to state that he believed what he did not really believe and he had to declare it with an oath. More was placed in prison. All kinds of pressures were put upon him to commit perjury. He was told that if he did not agree to the King's demands he would be put to death. His daughter Meg came to prison and pleaded with her father and begged him to sign the oath and save his life.

> More: You want me to swear to the Act of Succession?
> Margaret: "God more regards the thoughts of the heart than the words of the mouth." Or so you've always told me.
> More: Yes.
> Margaret: Then say the words of the oath and in your heart think otherwise.
> More: What is an oath then but words we say to God?
> Margaret: That's very neat.
> More: Do you mean it isn't true?
> Margaret: No, it's true.
> More: Then it's a poor argument to call it "neat," Meg. When a man takes an oath, Meg, he's holding his own self in his own hands. Like water. (He cups his hands). And if he opens his fingers then - he needn't hope to find himself again. Some men aren't capable of this, but I'd be loath to think your father one of them."[49]

We need more persons - men and women and young people who have high standards, strong convictions, and high moral values, who have modeled their lives after Christ and are not carried away by every wind of popular appeal and corruption that comes along. These are the people who have determined to let Christ be the standard for their lives and follow Him. This is not always easy. Many forces constantly pull at us.

---

49   Bolt, Robert. *A Man for All Seasons* (New York: Vintage Books, 1962), 81.

I heard about a woman who had lost her sense of touch. She could place her hand on a hot stove and be burned badly because she could not feel it. Her hand could be literally frozen to a block of ice because she could not feel the pain. A pin could be stuck in her hand and she could not feel it. That is a great tragedy and danger. What an even greater tragedy it would be for those of us who are supposed to be children of God, if we lose our sense of feeling for what is right and wrong. Injustice, immorality and unethical behavior are grossly evident in our land and around the world. We are challenged not only to do what is right and moral ourselves, but we must seek to see that justice and righteousness is directed and administered for all persons regardless of their race, sex or sexual preference, religion, creed, political alliance, economic status, belief or non-belief. "There is a giant tear in our 'single garment of destiny.' It cannot be repaired from one side only," exclaims Steve Boyd, John Allen Easley Professor of Religion at Wake Forest University. "To mend it will take many people—blacks and whites, Latinos, Native Americans, and Asians, Christians, Jews, Muslims, and non-believers, lay people, policy makers, lawyers and judges," he continues. "We need people who will make justice our business. We need those who will take up needle and thread, find people of peace and justice on the other side of the tear, and start sewing toward them."[50]

May Paul, in his words to the Corinthian church, remind us that we have been bought with a price and are consecrated to God, and therefore, are challenged to glorify God through our bodies. My prayer is that we not lose our personal sense of value for what is morally right and just for us but for all people as we strive daily to bear witness to the Christ we serve and follow in His call to the higher righteous way of His Kingdom.

---

50   Boyd, Stephen B. *Making Justice Our Business: The Wrongful Conviction of Darryl Hunt and the Work of Faith* (Eugene, Oregon: Cascade Books, 2011), 116. See also Will Willimon, *Who Lynched Willie Earle? Preaching to Confront Racism* (Nashville: Abingdon Press, 2017).

CHAPTER 9

THE CHURCH'S CALL TO ECOLOGICAL ACTION

Some voices today say that global warming and environmental concerns are not legitimate or are overstated. But several years ago, new prophets arose in the world and were perceiving apocalyptic visions which told of an impending environmental doomsday. These new prophets were not religious leaders but scientists called ecologists, persons who study the environment. Sounding strangely like Old Testament prophets, the ecological voices of doom are continuing to scream loudly to awaken a sleeping people to the consequences of transgressing the natural life systems and ignoring an ecological balance. By now humanity is keenly aware that this is more than alarmist talk. The devastation to our air, water and land is apparent. Humanity is guilty of raping the natural world, and his/her sin is open for all to see. Is redemption still possible?

A popular adage states, "If you're not part of the solution, then you're part of the pollution." Can we ignore these voices and not trust the voice of environmental scientists? Does the church have any role to play in this dilemma or should it sit idly by and assume that science and technology will take the initiative? Ecologists have demonstrated that there is a strong link between population, productivity, and pollution. Technology has dug deeply into natural resources to meet the demands of an ever-increasing population, and without guidance and control it can become a Frankenstein monster which may soon turn on its inventor. Technology can provide solutions for many of the specific environmental problems, if it receives the necessary social and political stimuli to influence its goals. As good and necessary as these technological strivings may be for the environment, they will not provide a permanent cure. Technology is dealing with the symptoms of a deeper disease, the ruthless exploitation of the environment. This necessitates probing beyond the external symptoms to reach the causes which have precipitated the ecological crisis. William Ernest "Bill" McKibben, the Schumann Distinguished Scholar at Middlebury College and leader of the anti-carbon campaign group, 350.org, is an American environmentalist, author, and journalist who has written extensively on the impact of global warming. He has authored a dozen books about the environment, including his first, *The End of Nature*, which focused on climate change. In his recent book, *Eaarth: Making a Life on a Tough New Planet*, McKibben observes that the earth changes constantly but we are, he believes, in "change far larger and more thorough going than anything we can read in the record of rocks and ice."[51] It is so severe that he uses a new term for our planet—Eaarth. The National Oceanic and Atmospheric Administration released a statement in the beginning of 2017 that their study shows that global warming is continuing.[52]

What is essential for an effective, lasting solution is a revolution — a revolution in attitude and practice. Of all the institutions in society today, the church needs to be the prophetic voice in the midst of its people, challenging them to be aware of their sins against the natural world and seek atonement with God's creation. The church is primarily concerned with changing lives, attitudes, and values. It must assume the responsibility for being the catalyst to revolutionize the values and attitudes of humanity if the environmental destruction is to be arrested. The church will not find this an easy task, since it is often the taillight and not the headlight in the contemporary world. The handwriting is on the wall, however, and the church must accept its responsibility to proclaim the word. Will we hear it cry?

---

51 McKibben, Bill. *Eaarth: Making a Life on a Tough New Planet* (New York: Times Books, 2010), 3.
52 "Study Shows Global Warming Continuing," Richmond Times-Dispatch (January 5, 2017), 7.

STEP I. A THEOLOGICAL AND ETHICAL BASE

Some ecologists have asserted that the environmental crisis is basically an ethical and moral problem. Lynn White, Jr., observed that modern science and technology are so tainted with an "orthodox Christian arrogance toward nature" that the solution to the pollution crisis is fundamentally religious. "Since the roots of our trouble are so largely religious, the remedy must also be essentially religious, whether we call it that or not."[53] Technological modifications alone cannot solve the problem since the very foundations of a style of life are at issue here. The church needs to provide some guidelines for action to bring about a change of mind and attitude. The following brief suggestions are projected as guidelines which a church might utilize in seeking to confront the ecological crisis. Since values and attitudes are the fundamental cause, the church must first begin by laying a proper theological and ethical base to correct distorted environmental concepts. The church needs to provide a theology of ecology. The second step I suggest will focus on practical ways the church can engage its members in being a part of the solution and less a part of the deterioration of the environment.

HUMANITY: RESPONSIBLE CARETAKER NOT RUTHLESS OWNER

If the church is going to change values, it must begin with the challenge which it finds on its own doorstep. Some scientists have placed the blame for humanity's carelessness and spirit of exploitation on the Judea-Christian tradition, and have interpreted this tradition to affirm that man/woman owns the earth and is unrestricted in his/her use of it. Rene Dubos reflects on man's saga of conquest: "The American way of life, now spreading all over the world, is based on the myth that man is the Lord of Creation. This has become a credo and almost a religion of the world's

---

53   White, Jr., Lynn. "The Historical Roots of Our Ecologic Crisis," *The Environmental Handbook,* ed. Garrett de Bell (New York: Ballantine Books, 1970), 26.

masses and their leaders."[54] Lynn White, Jr., Richard Means, Paul L. Ehrlich and others pointed decades ago, in a similar fashion, to the traditional Christian heritage as the force which has established within our culture an attitude that depicts humanity's role as dominating nature, rather than living in harmony with it.

The creation narratives found in Genesis do focus on man/woman, and Genesis 1:28 cannot be eluded: "Be fruitful and multiply, and fill the earth and subdue it; and have dominion over the fish of the sea and over the birds of the air and over every living thing that moves upon the earth." The church needs to demonstrate that the biblical tradition, however, has much more to say about humanity's relationship to nature than is found in one isolated verse. "Adam," humanity, is not depicted as lord of creation in his own right but is instructed, as recorded in the second creation story, to till and keep the garden in which he is placed (Genesis 2:15). Humanity needs to be reminded that it has only a delegated dominion and is lord of creation only as he/she acts as a steward responsible to God (Psalm 24:1). Humanity's limited dominion and respect for nature is often revealed in restrictions on its relationship to cattle, birds, wildlife, land, and crops (cf. Deuteronomy 22:9-11, 25:4; Leviticus 19:19; Exodus 23:10; Psalm 12:10). In a total biblical perspective humanity is seen not only as an overlord but *as a* caretaker who seeks to enhance and defend nature's balance.

A RENEWED AWARENESS OF AESTHETICS

Whenever the church attempts to call humanity back to an awareness of the aesthetic value of nature, one can hear cries of "nature worship" and sense fears of romanticizing the simple "rustic life." American writers such as Ralph Waldo Emerson, Henry David Thoreau, James Fennimore Cooper, Hal Borland, and the naturalist, John Muir, helped to popularize an adoration for the world of nature, often set in opposition to the cities and the "prog-

---

54   Dubos, Rene'. *"Man and His Environment: Adaptations and Interactions: The Fitness of Man's Environment,"* *Smithsonian Annual;* II), (Washington, D.C.: Smithsonian Institution Press, 1968), 243-4.

ress" of humanity. Over against this, the church needs to establish a biblical appreciation for the authentic wonder, awe, mystery, joy, praise, and beauty revealed within and through the natural order. The church, by its nature, is often concerned with aspects of humanity's life that are not always verifiable by empirical data and sensory perception. Modern humanity's aesthetic value has often been directed toward an appreciation of what humanity has created in concrete, steel, plastic, glass, etc., instead of sensing the beauty within the earth itself. The church has opportunity to set humanity attuned again to the natural world, A sense of the beautiful can help nourish the deeper needs of humanity's being which go beyond the tangible demands. Harrison Brown has detected this dimension of life: "The flower and vegetable garden, green grass, the fireplace, the primeval forest with its wondrous assemblage of living things, the uninhabited hilltop where one can silently look at the stars and wonder - all of these things and many others are necessary for the fulfillment of man's psychological and spiritual needs."[55]

The church finds itself on strong biblical grounds when it affirms the aesthetic value of nature. The Psalms are filled with references to the glory and mystery of creation. Psalms 8:19: 1-6:24; 29:104 are most expressive, while Job 37-41 is deeply profound in its praise of the wonders of the created realm. The biblical writers conceive of the whole of nature as having value and significance in itself for God and see it not merely as *a* stage upon which humanity lives. The order and beauty of nature are "delights" (Psalm 104:31; Proverbs 8:30) to a Creator who sees God's creation as "very good" (Genesis 1:31). When man/woman seeks to relate in an authentic way to nature, he/she senses its beauty and responds, like H. Paul Santmire has depicted, as a "wondering onlooker," who moves from wonder to a celebration of the sense of the presence of God.[56] Loren Eiseley, the noted anthropologist of several decades ago, has been

---

55 Brown, Harrison. The *Challenge of Man's Future.* (New York: Viking Press, Compass Books, 1956), 257- 258.

56 Santmire, H. Paul. *Brother Earth: Nature God and Ecology in Time of Crisis.* (New York: Thomas Nelson, Inc., 1970), 190.

described by Frederick Elder as one who is more than a naturalist and anthropologist in his study of nature but is seen as a person who has what Rudolf Otto called an "awareness of the numinous." Elder has detected in Eiseley the deeper implications involved in an authentic awareness of the aesthetics of nature. Referring to Eiseley, Elder notes: "Viewing nature, he sees not only empirical interrelatedness and he senses not only aesthetic enjoyment, but he also perceives in it and through it the holy, the miraculous — that awesomeness which has marked religious consciousness from the beginning."[57] The church needs to help re-establish this kind of value appreciation.

AN ECOLOGICAL CONSCIOUSNESS

Although the church has often been the echo and reflection of a larger community, its prophetic role as the conscience of society is one of its truest functions. Religious concern cannot be merely for personal redemption but must envision a wider scope to include what Walter Rauschenbusch called "the super-personal forces of evil"[58] in society. The church must speak in opposition to humanity's sins against the environment and warn that this continued abuse threatens to upset the harmony of the earth. "The church is the social factor in salvation." Rauschenbusch observed over fifty years ago, "It brings social forces to bear on evil."[59] The church has opportunity to confront technological man/woman as the ecological conscience of society and seek to replace the frontier mentality toward the earth's resources with an environmental ethic that sees humanity rightfully as a steward and custodian, not owner and master. Humanity's basic sin against the environment has been the attitude of exploitation, the growth philosophy which always demands increased production, consumption, and expansion. The

---

57   Elder, Frederick. *Crisis in Eden: A Religious Study of Man and Environment.* (Nashville: Abingdon Press, 1970). 15.

58   Rauschenbusch, Walter. A *Theology for the Social Gospel* (New York: The Macmillan Co., 1917). 69f.

59   Ibid., 119.

problem before humanity today is not simply a question of morality or conscience but one of survival. What is needed, then, is a different value perspective in which technological humanity makes an ethical covenant with the earth. It is, therefore, ultimately a question of the will. Greed and selfishness can blind humanity from finding redemptive healing, or she/he can discover not only the "fatherhood of God" and the "brotherhood of humanity" but the "sisterhood of the biosphere" as well. As the social factor in redemption, the church assumes its role as the pressure force in society to guide humanity to make peace with the earth.

Pope Francis's encyclical, *Laudato Si',* released on June 19, 2015 made a passionate call "to every person living on the planet" to respond to the reality of climate change as "one of the principal challenges facing humanity in our day." He rebuffed the arguments of climate skeptics and challenged the interpretation of those who used the book of Genesis wording that is frequently quoted to denote man's "dominion" over the Earth, and hence exploitation of its resources for our selfish needs. Pope Francis is unequivocal in the encyclical that "this is not a correct interpretation of the Bible as understood by the church." He declared that we must respect the laws of nature and protect the Earth for future generations. Humans are part of nature, not its overlords, he affirms, and caring for ourselves and for nature is inseparable in caring for our common home.[60] Whether we are Catholics or Protestants or of no religious tradition, his argument strikes home. In February 2006, eighty-six Christian leaders, who were so vitally concerned about climate change, formed what was called the "Evangelical Climate Initiative" and demanded that Congress regulate greenhouse gases.[61] In his book, *Our Endangered Values: America's Moral Crisis,* former

60 www.theguardian.com *"Exegesis of Pope Francis's encyclical call for action on climate change."*
    To read the encyclical see: http://w2.vatican.va/content/francesco/en/encyclical/documents/papafrancesco_20150524_enciclica-laudato-si.html.
61 Kluger, Jeffrey. "By Any Measure, Earth Is at the Tipping Point," *Time* (April 3, 2006), 35.

president, Jimmy Carter, in addressing the major threats to the environment declared boldly: "Our proper stewardship of God's world is a personal and political moral commitment."[62]

We can't just keep on abusing, and destroying rain forests and other parts of the natural world without bringing devastation upon ourselves and our world. Some have a dim view of environmentalists and pretend that we do not have a serious problem But, it is serious! Denying global warming and pretending climate change is not happening is like "sticking our head" in the sand. We must realize that our children and grandchildren and others may not be able to live in our world unless we take care of it. *National Geographic* devoted the September 2004 issue to "Global Warming" and warned that "the climate is changing at an unnerving pace. Glaciers are retreating, ice shelves are fracturing, sea level is rising, permafrost is melting."[63] The April 3, 2006 issue of *Time* magazine was entitled "Special Report Global Warming," and warned that "climate change isn't some vague future problem—it's already damaging the planet at an alarming pace."[64] George Philander, professor of geosciences at Princeton, declares that there are many aspects of global warming that are still only dimly understood by scientists. He acknowledges that humanity is disturbing the natural cycles which we really do not understand very well. It's like; he projects, being in "a ship in the fog in treacherous waters…. We should be doing something, not because we know what's going to happen, but because we don't know what's going to happen."[65] The December 28, 2016/January 2, 2017 issue of *Time* wrote about thousands of people protesting in the streets of New Delhi about the awful pollution in their city and how their air pollution was

---

62 Carter, Jimmy. *Our Endangered Values: America's Moral Crisis* (New York: Simon & Schuster, 2005), 177.

63 Glick, Daniel. "The Big Thaw," *National Geographic* (September 2004), 13.

64 *Time*, (April 3, 2006), front cover.

65 Flanagan, Eileen. "Temperature Rising," *The Christian Century* (August 21, 2013), 26.

getting worse.[66] Hopefully, the Clean Air Act, the Clean Water Act, the Clean Power Plan, and the recent Paris Climate Accord will continue to be enforced by the EPA.

The conservationist, Aldo Leopold, was one of the first to argue for an "ecological conscience." He observed that ethical systems had depicted the relation between individuals; individuals and society; and even social organizations to the individuals, but he saw the need for a "land ethic." "There is yet no ethic dealing with man's relation to land and to animals and plants which grow upon it .... The extension of ethics to this third element in human environment is, if I read the evidence correctly, an evolutionary possibility and an ecological necessity."[67] Society cannot assume that the government and technology will immediately shoulder its responsibility without pressure coming to bear upon them. Technology, society, and the government must feel the constant pressure of the church demanding an ecological awareness by all persons.

REVERENCE FOR LIFE

The ecological problem may have forced us to heed voices that have sounded strange in calmer times. The teaching of reverence for all life, both lower and higher forms, championed centuries ago by Francis of Assisi, has been presented forcefully in the writings of Albert Schweitzer. Instead of an attitude of careless destruction of life, reverence for all life, if emphasized by the church, would challenge all persons to respect and appreciate all forms of life. This ethic might emerge as a factor to overcome the frontier, consumptive mentality. Francis and Schweitzer could provide many churches with fruitful book studies, guidelines, and dialogue. The teaching of Reverence for Life can furnish the church with some theological moorings in the midst of the environmental tempest. "The essence of Goodness is:" Schweitzer observed, "preserve life,

---

66 Worland, Justin. "How Bad Air Came Back," *Time* (December 28, 2016/ January 2, 2017), 94-95.

67 Leopold, Aldo. *A Sand County Almanac* (New York: Oxford University Press, 1966}, 218.

promote life, help life to achieve its highest destiny. The essence of Evil is: Destroy life, harm life, hamper the development of life."[68]

AT-ONE-MENT

Man/woman is apart from nature and, nevertheless, is a part of nature. Whatever humanity does to the natural environment ultimately affects us as well. All of life is tied together in a web of life. Rauschenbusch reminded the church of the solidarity of humanity when he observed that "Sin is not a private transaction between the sinner and God. Humanity always crowds the audience-room when God holds court."[69] Ecologists are reminding humanity today of the solidarity not only of humankind but of all living things. Cutting our forests, using DDT, pouring waste and pollutants into our air and streams, the spread of concrete cities and highways, touch all of life. Lewis Mumford expressed humanity's dilemma when he wrote: "Though he (she) is now the dominant species, his (her) fate is still bound up with the prosperity of all forms of life."[70]

Man/woman will find atonement with nature when he/she comes to the awareness that one's ecological salvation depends upon his/her cooperation with the natural order. Atonement will be realized ecologically when we see ourselves as intimately connected with all life, and whatever we do either conserves or diminishes life for all. As God's caretaker, we are obligated to abide by both the natural as well as the moral laws of the Creator. The church also needs to attest that the redemptive process is concerned not only with humanity but with all of creation which is itself moving toward fulfillment. "The creation itself will be set free from its bondage to decay and obtain the glorious liberty *of* the children of God" (Romans 8:21. cf. 1 Corinthians 15:28; Romans 11:36; Revelation 21:1).

---

68 Schweitzer, Albert. *The Teaching of Reverence for Life* (New York: Holt, Rinehart, and Winston, 1965), 26.

69 Rauschenbusch, *op. cit.,* 48.

70 Mumford, Lewis. *The Transformations of Man* (New York: Collier Books, 1956), 2.

RESPONSIBLE POPULATION CONTROL

If the church has any power to modify values and attitudes, the population problem demands full and immediate attention. Many of the ecological problems stem from, or are aggravated by, the swelling numbers around the world. Scientists have projected that it took mankind nearly a million years to reach the first billion by about 1850. With incredible speed the second billion was reached in the 1920's. In 1975, we reached 4 billion. By 2000, the figure was projected to be 6.3 billion.[71] The "population explosion" has caused many of the ecologists to predict that mankind has only about thirty-five years left on this planet.

The population explosion must be stopped. This will entail a radical change in the mores and values of our society. When America was much smaller and rural in orientation, large families may have been an economic necessity, but today they are a threat to the very survival of mankind. A zero-growth rate in the population, ecologist insists, is essential. This means that each new family should limit the size of its family to two children. Americans often assume that it is the poor of the world who have so many children and are the greatest polluters. But studies have indicated that one American uses more of the resources of the earth than fifty Indian children. The affluent nations, with their advanced technology, make the biggest demands on earth's systems. The former Stanford University biologist Paul Ehrlich predicted that if birth control is not practiced on a worldwide scale, famine, plague, and nuclear war will be the consequences. Pogo, the comic strip hero of Okefenokee swamp, observed that "we have met the enemy, and he is us." Exactly! The church can champion the cause of population control and use its resources to change the concept of the "blessings" of large families to the absolute necessity for responsible birth control and limited-size families. The church in challenging the present folkways can provide an "ethic of reproduction" which will help

---

71 Clark, Susan J. *Celebrating Earth Holy Days*, (New York: Crossroads, 1992), 50.

stabilize the population and make it less of a burden to the natural resources.

STEP II. SOME PRACTICAL GUIDELINES FOR CHURCH ACTION

If the church is to be the conscience of society, it ought to be the "pilot plant" which exhibits through its teachings and ministry a set of values and goals adequate for the ecological crisis. Through its preaching and teaching the church can attempt to lay *a* strong theological base to reorient humanity for proper living in today's world.. Instead of despair or apathy the church must resolve to become involved in the revolution to combat the ecological problems. It is easy to despair and it is easy to do nothing. Sometimes the ecological problems may seem so awesome that one is tempted to say: "Why bother? We can't do anything about it." "The great enemy of morality," Schweitzer reminds us, "has always been indifference."[72] An apathetic people cannot engender the solution. Only those who are keenly aware of the value of all life will help solve the problem of the environmental crisis as they strive to contribute their service toward its solution. The following methods may help to implement these concerns:

(1) Organize *Bible study groups* or use some of the regular church organizations to engage in a detailed analysis of the biblical relationship of humanity and the environment. Include in this study an examination of the Genesis creation narratives, some of the Psalms, Job 37-41, Romans 8:19-24 and others which might be suggested in your parallel reading. *Genesis 1-11, The Creation Stories and the Modern World View* by Alan Richardson, commentaries and Old Testament Theologies, especially by Walter Eichrodt and Gerhard von Rad, among others, will be useful. Attention can also be given to the biblical concept of aesthetics, covenant, responsibility, and redemption.

---

72 Schweitzer, *op. cit.,* 119.

(2) *Book Study Groups* can be formed to examine various aspects of the ecology problem. One group might consider ecological classics such as the following: Rene *Dubos, So Human an Animal;* Rachel Carson, *Silent Spring:* Loren Eiseley, *Immense Journey;* Aldo Leopold, *Sand County Almanac;* and Fairfield Osborn, *Our Plundered Planet.* Another group might concern itself with theological approaches to the environment by studying some of the following: Denis Edwards, *Jesus and the Cosmos*; Conrad Honifazi, *A Theology of Things;* Teilhard de Chardin, *Building the Earth;* Frederick Elder, *Crisis in Eden;* Donald Imsland, *Celebrate the Earth;* E. C. Rust, *Nature: Garden or Desert?* and H. Paul Santmire, *Brother Earth.* Discussion groups may find thoughtful stimulation from such books as Bill McKibben, *Eaarth* and *End of Nature*; Joseph Ramm, *Climate Change: What Everyone Needs to Know;* Dana Nuccitelli, *Climatology Versus Pseudoscience*; Michael E. Mann, *The Hockey Stick and the Climate Wars*; Al Gore, *Our Choice: A Plan to Solve the Climate Crisis;* H. Paul Firnhaber, *Earth Care Manual;* *Can Man Care for the Earth?* edited by Richard L. Heiss and Noel F. Mcinnis, and Donald A. Williams, et al., *Christians and the Good Earth.* Two excellent children's books include *Please Don't Paint the Planet Pink* by Gregg Kleiner and *Climate Change: Discover How It Impacts Spaceship Earth* (with 25 projects) by Erin Twamley and Joshua Sneiderman.

(3) A carefully planned *Ecological Symposium* would provide opportunity for a church to engage not only its own membership in a serious look at the environmental crisis, but its impact could possibly be felt in the whole community. One of the area colleges will almost certainly have a science professor who is deeply concerned about the crisis, and he or she can present some of the scientific problems in the pollution malady. Many cities have Pollution Control Centers which might be able to suggest speakers. Several of our seminaries have professors who have given a great deal of attention to the theological and ethical aspects of the problem and they could share many helpful insights. Other speakers could be attained from conservation organizations and other nature

societies. Films might be used not only to provide visual reference to the problems, but they could also stimulate group discussions. Businessmen from local industries could be invited to share what, if anything, their industry is doing to control its pollution. Drama, book studies, reviews as well as sermons and class teaching would attempt to focus the attention of the church and community on the problem. The Sunday morning sermon could begin the special study, with possible Sunday nights or a week night being devoted to a panel of speakers on the issue with dialogue following. The series could continue through Wednesday night or longer, if desired, with each night focusing on some phase of the pollution problem using a panel, speaker, film, drama, or a combination of these. If the church budget will allow, nationally recognized ecologists could be invited to speak. A church and one or several of the local colleges might plan to use his or her services and share the expenses. Many variations are possible in this type of program.

(4) *A Film Festival* would provide a dramatic medium for the presentation of various areas of the ecological problem. A list of films can be found on the web site "Green Films: The Best Environmental Documentaries." Several good films to examine include the following: *Cross of the Moment, Revolution, Earth: An Incontinent Truth, Forget Shorter Showers, Unacceptable Levels,* and *Blind Spots.* The films not only provide helpful information but are excellent discussion starters.

(5) Any realistic effort by the church to confront this issue will entail a program in *family planning and birth control.* This study needs to provide not only sexual knowledge to the young, but classes that will teach the need for population control and various birth control methods. Each church can determine the best way to conduct these classes in its own situation, but areas of consideration should include: the critical nature of the population explosion, planned parenthood and Zero Population Growth, abortion, sterilization (vasectomy for the male and tubal ligation for the female), the possibility of eliminating tax deductions for more than two children, adoption, etc. Paul R. Ehrlich's book, *The*

Population Bomb, demands careful study. This program could be entitled "Responsible Family Planning" and used for a quarter's study in the Christian Education School for young married couples and others, or be a special unit of study over a period of months. Local physicians, marriage counselors, science teachers, and ministers might possibly staff this program.

(6) Form a local church group composed of those who are seriously interested in the question of pollution. The group could be called *CARE,* "The Church Against Ravaging the Environment." Part of the aim of this group should be to inform and educate your church and community about the local, national, and worldwide ecological problems. Search your own community and isolate the causes of pollution. Inquire if any local or national organizations, such as the Izsaak Walton League, Pollution Control Centers, the Audubon Society, and the Sierra Club, are already working to combat these problems. If they are working, find ways to join them. If no one is doing anything, assign different members the responsibility of finding out what local, state or national laws may exist to deter pollution.

When you determine what the local problems are, establish a campaign to inform your church and community of the situation. Contact and inform your neighbors, schools, industries, city council, mayor, senators, and governor, and apprise them of problems. Urge that action be taken to remedy the pollution violations. Be aware that you may have to write letters, send emails, texts, telephone, vote, get petitions signed, speak before civic groups, or use TV or radio time to plead your case before the community. Any alert person might ask what can one person really do? John W. Gardner has responded to that question: "If any substantial number continue to believe that one man can do *a* great deal, then they will preserve a system that sustains their belief."[73] A chemical firm in West Elizabeth, Pennsylvania was convicted, some years ago, for violating the 1899 Rivers and Harbors Act. This conviction

---

73 Gardner, John W. *The Recovery of Confidence* (New York: W.W. Norton & Co., 1970), 141.

was the first in the United States obtained in a jury trial based on information furnished by citizens.[74] Reports of what many groups, both large and small, have done to arouse their communities to the problems and the results that were attained have been carried in many news magazines.[75]

This group of aroused citizens can also demand that new and more rigid laws he enacted to control and prevent pollution. The Federal Air Quality Act has been one attempt to establish air-purity standards. Stronger laws, however, are not enough; they must be enforced. Be willing to turn to the courts and bring suits as individuals or groups against those who ravage our environment,[76]

(7) Study what can be done on an individual basis by examining such works as *The Everyman 's Guide to Ecological Living*, by Greg Cailliet, et al.; *How to Live in Our Polluted World*, by May Bethel; *The User's Guide to the Protection of the Environment*, by Paul Swatek; and Judith S. Scherff's, *The Mother Earth Handbook*. These works discuss such things as good buying practices, the least polluting detergent pesticides, packaging, and the best ways to conserve water, land, and air. Ideas and suggestions are found here that every home and church can use.

(8) For special youth or church projects, guide the organizations to consider forming clean-up campaigns to pick up old newspapers, glass bottles, aluminum cans and other items and turn them in to the respective recycling Centers. Instruction concerning either organizing or conducting these drives are given in *Everyman's Guide to Ecological Living*. This little book can prove to be a most helpful study guide.

Can we shut our ears to the agonizing cries from our environment itself? I believe that to ignore these cries leads to a pathway of doom. But the Christian believes in hope. Although the envi-

---

74   *The Nashville Tennessean*, July 1, 1971.

75   See, for example, Life, January 30, 1970; *Time*, February 2, 1970; *U.S. News & World Report*, February 9, 1970.

76   One example is "DuPont to pay $50M for river pollution in VA," *Richmond Times-Dispatch* (December 16, 2016), 1.

ronmental situation is critical, the Christian Church still proclaims the possibility of atonement, if men and women will repent and live in harmony with the Creator and God's creation. One of the ecological prophets, Barry Commoner, has declared that we are in a period of grace. We have the time — perhaps a generation-in which to save the environment from the final effects of the violence humanity has done to it. And Jesus said: "He that hath ears to hear, let him hear." (Matthew 11:15)

CHAPTER 10

THE BIBLE AS OUR SPIRITUAL GUIDE

A Roman legend records that Sibyl of Cumae offered to sell the King of Tarquin nine volumes in which she had gathered all the wisdom of the world. The king felt that her price was too high and refused to buy them. She burned three of the volumes and offered to sell the six for the same price she had asked originally for nine. He still said no. She burned three more, and offered him the remaining three at the same price she had asked originally for the nine. This time, fearful that all the volumes containing the wisdom would be lost, he purchased the remaining volumes.

In some ways this story is a reminder of how we often approach the Bible. The wisdom of the ages is found within its covers. Words that describe man and woman's relationship to God, how to relate to one another, and how God has loved and redeemed us. But in our youth we do not take time to read them and their wisdom is lost to us. In middle age and sometimes even in old age, the offer to read the wisdom is unheeded. We have lost our opportunity again. The price is still the same. It requires, at any age, time, attention, study, and reading.

A NEGLECTED BOOK

Why is it that we often do not read the Bible which is supposed to be the Church's chief source book? There is no question today that the Bible is indeed a neglected book. Yet, almost all homes in America seem to have Bibles today. The Bible is still a national best seller. But what is the Bible used for by these people who purchase it? Well, it is filled with clippings, roses are pressed in it, pictures of children, grandchildren or relatives are kept there. It sits on our table like some kind of magic talisman, but it almost never gets read, except on rare, special occasions. It is a neglected book. In a 2017 survey of 1000 Americans, *Life Way Research* found that about half of Americans (53 percent) have read relative little of the Bible. One in ten has read none of it. Thirteen percent indicate that they have read only a few sentences. Thirty percent state that they have read a few passages or stories. Eleven percent declare that they have read the entire Bible through at least once; while nine percent declare that they have read the Bible through multiple times.[77]

SOME CALL IT DULL

Some say, "The Bible is so dull!" It is even dull in its appearance with its dark black or blue cover, its narrow parallel columns and small print. Some say, "I've tried to read it, but it's impossible to understand, and even if you understand it, I don't find it very interesting." So many simply do not read it.

Some airplane passengers have learned that they can avoid conversation with others on the plane by carrying a Bible with them. I heard about a traveling salesman, who simply gets on airplanes, opens a Bible and puts it on his lap, and nobody ever bothers him. He found that people quickly lost interest in talking with him, if he flexed a Bible.

UNFAMILIAR TO MANY

The Bible is also very unfamiliar to us. The Bible is, to use Bruce Barton's phrase, "The Book nobody knows." If I asked you to look up the Book of Hezekiah, I expect many of you might start searching for that book. But there is no such book in the Bible. It just sounds like it ought to be. Many of us are like the young man who said, "I don't understand all this conversation about Dan and Beersheba. I thought they were husband and wife just like Sodom and Gomorrah." Now, if you don't find that story humorous, it indicates something of the nature of the problem we have in studying

---

77 Smietana, Bob. "How Much of the Bible Have You Personally Read?" *LifeWayResearch.com*, (April 25, 2017).

the Bible. Most people are honestly not familiar with the contents of the Scriptures. Many feel that the Bible is filled with strange books. Why, there are stories in the book of Revelation about a scarlet woman, a great beast, and all of those crazy numbers and names that people have tried to understand for centuries. Who knows what they really mean? The Old Testament is filled with discussions about ancient tribal rights and sacrificial systems. Who in the world can read with much satisfaction through the begats and all the genealogies? Do you really enjoy reading about "who begat whom?" That's not fantastic devotional reading. But, in a few places, the list goes on page after page. As Karl Barth says, "There is a strange new world within the Bible," and we might add, many never discover it.

The only place many people ever hear Scripture read at all is in a Sunday morning worship service or in a funeral service. When the Scripture is read in some Protestant traditions, the minister may say, "This is the word of God." In some congregations they respond, "Thanks be to God." But many today are not really too thankful for the Scriptures, are they? If we were, we would spend more time reading and studying them. In spite of that fact, the Bible continues to be the Church's chief authoritative source, as it has been down through its history. The Bible is authoritative to us because it has guided us into our understanding of God, his redemption, grace, and how we are to relate to other persons. It is our primary source for understanding Christ, his Church, the history of Israel, and our Christian doctrines.

THE SCRIPTURES ARE INSPIRED

Unfortunately, there are some who have equated biblical authority with inerrancy and infallibility. But inerrancy and in-fallibility are non-biblical words. They are not found within the Scriptures. They are interpretations of Scripture. They are some-body's theological concepts which are bought from outside the Bible and pressed upon the Scriptures as one way to understand

them. Paul writes in Timothy that "all scripture is given by inspiration" (2 Timothy 3:16). It is "God breathed." But technically he
is writing about the Old Testament. When Paul wrote his letter to
Timothy he wasn't talking about his letters. The gospels had not
been written. He was referring to the Old Testament writings. He
never dreamed that his letters would be put together as part of a
book called the New Testament. When Paul wrote that "the Word
of God is not bound" (2 Timothy 2:9), he was not writing about
the Bible. He was writing about the "Word of Jesus Christ" — the
living Word of God. This "Word" can never be bound.

The "Word" which Isaiah proclaimed is the "Word" that has
continued through the decades as God has bombarded the hearts of
men and women to inform them of his will and way. "My word,"
Isaiah declared, "shall not return unto me void, but it shall accomplish that which I please, and it shall prosper in the thing whereto
I send it" (Isaiah 55:11). Moffatt translates this phrase, "It carries
out my purpose." God's Word is actively bringing about his will
in the lives of men and women.

THE FOCUS OF SCRIPTURE

Isn't it strange that the reformation under the guidance of
Luther and Calvin, moved us away from an infallible church, and
today we have others who are trying to establish an infallible book
as the Church's authoritative source. If we mean by infallible what
it meant originally, "that which cannot fall or fail," then the Scriptures are infallible. They do not fall nor fail in revealing God's love
and redemption. But if anyone tries to assert that the Scriptures
are inerrant in science, medicine, or history, he or she does not
understand the nature or composition of the Bible.

The Scriptures are pre-scientific. In the Old Testament, there
are references to a flat earth supported on pillars with a dome cov-
ering it. This is a pre-scientific description of our world. Does that
mean that we must believe that the earth has four corners? Do we
take the Bible literally and believe in a flat earth? Of course, not.

It was pre-science. There are one hundred fifty thousand variations which have been found in ancient biblical tests. If they are inerrant, why shouldn't they all read the same way?

If the original autographs were inerrant, why did God not preserve them? If they are essential to our understanding of the Bible, why did God allow them to become lost? Does this mean that our Bible today is not dependable? We have to remember that the persons who wrote the Scriptures were ordinary men who did not lose their humanity when they were inspired by God. They were not robots but real human persons and subject to human error.

Turn to the gospels and read the inscription nailed to the cross of Jesus. Each one is slightly different. If the Bible is inerrant, they should have exactly the same words. The Gospel of John records that Jesus cleansed the temple at the beginning of his ministry. But Matthew, Mark, and Luke state that it was at the end of his ministry. These kinds of variations are to be expected when human persons rely on their memory. Each writer reflected on what he had seen or heard. It is not essential that the words of the Bible be inerrant to be meaningful. It doesn't change the revelation of God's message of redemptive love and grace one iota. That is constant.

ALL THE BIBLE IS NOT LITERAL

Marcus Borg has challenged our modern world to view the Bible through a new lens of interpretation in his book, *Reading the Bible Again for the First Time*. In reading the Bible, we are being led, he asserts, to "a deepening relationship with the God to whom the Bible points, lived within the Christian tradition as a sacrament of the sacred."[78] All the Bible is not written to be taken literally. Jesus is not literally a door or a shepherd. These are figures of speech as any reasonable person can see. To take all of the Bible literally is not to take it seriously. We also cannot put all Scripture on the same level. We do not have a flat Bible where every passage is on the same level with another. The Bible is not a strange collection

78 Borg, Marcus J. *Reading the Bible Again for the First Time* (San Francisco: Harper Collins, 2001), 158.

of proof-texts where one can dip down in any place she or he likes. Psalm 137:9 which reads, "Happy is the man who shall seize your children and dash them against the rock" is not on the same level with the words of Jesus, "Love your enemies." All Scripture is judged by the highest revelation we have — Jesus Christ. He is the final test. The Living Word judges the written word. The Bible is, to use Luther's phrase, "The Manger of Christ."

STRANGE INTERPRETATIONS

Some people have made the Scriptures a vast allegory. They have turned the Song of Song, which is a majestic love poem of a man for his wife, into a story about Christ and his Church. This was not the original writer's intent. Others have dipped down into the Book of Daniel and Revelation and have found there a picture of every contemporary international villain, especially from Communist countries, they could possibly discover. Rather than trying to see what the original writer was trying to describe for his day, they have fantasized images for our day. Even writers like Augustine turned the parable of the Good Samaritan into an allegory. A hidden meaning was read into every detail. "A certain man" was Adam. Jerusalem was the heavenly city. The robbers were the devil and his angels. The Samaritan was Jesus; the inn was the Church; the innkeeper was the Apostle Paul, and so forth. Rather than being a parable about relating to others in Christian love, this story became an allegory about the Christian doctrine of salvation.

CHIEF SOURCE OF AUTHORITY

In spite of the nonsensical things some have written and said about the Bible, that book continues to remain the chief source of authority for the Church. Through it God continues to speak his message of love, grace, and redemption to us. The Bible enriches our life because it came to birth out of the life of people. Its primary concern is not with abstract speculation or obscure thinking but with life itself. There are sixty-six different books in the Bible

— thirty-nine in the Old Testament and twenty-seven in the New Testament. The oldest book was written probably around 1300 B.C. The other books were written over a period of about fifteen hundred years. The books in the Bible were written and collected over a long period of time. They did not fall out of the sky one day or suddenly appear. The Bible records the story of the struggle of men and women to find meaning and purpose in their lives. It traces the story of the nation Israel and its struggle to become free from bondage, its birth as a nation, their difficulties in being God's people, their defeats and victories, their sins and accomplishments, their frustrations and needs.

A LIVING BOOK

Everywhere you touch the Bible it reverberates with life. It sobs with the pain of Job, the rejection of Jeremiah, the hope of Isaiah, the frustration of Jonah, the sin of David, the fulfillment of God's promise to make a Covenant with Israel, the hatred of a psalmist, the security of another psalmist, the courage of Queen Esther, the challenge of Amos, the doubt of Thomas, the promise of John, the faith of Paul, the failure and forgiveness of Peter, the grace of God and the hope of eternal life. The gospels tell about Jesus' birth, life, teachings, miracles, death and resurrection and the establishment of his Church. Paul's letters and the rest of the New Testament are a record of the beginning of the early Church.

What a marvelous book. It is both a human and divine book. It is human because God worked through ordinary people to bring it into existence. He worked through their gifts and personalities to convey his message. It is divine, because it is the record of God's relationship to humanity. It conveys his message to us today. It continues to provide us our guide for living and understanding God and Jesus.

Once a mechanic had been called to a famous observatory to repair one of their giant telescopes. When he took his lunch break, he sat down and read his Bible for a while. When one of the astronomers saw him doing that, he asked: "What good do you expect from that? The Bible is out of date; you don't even know who wrote it." The mechanic paused for a moment and then observed: "Don't you make considerable use of the multiplication table in your calculation?" "Why, yes, of course," the astronomer replied. "Do you know who wrote it?" "Why, no, I guess I don't." "Then," the mechanic asked, "how can you trust the multiplication table?" "We trust it because," he responded, "well, because it works." "Well," the mechanic replied, "I trust the Bible for the same reason; it just works."

Through the centuries, the Bible has nourished the life of the Church. Let's quit wrestling with words like inerrancy and infallibility and making them a test of faith and get back to the Scriptures themselves. The Word of God will not fall to the ground, because it is a living Word that still changes those whom it touches today. Rather than arguing about the Bible, it is more important to study it and learn from it.

I want to suggest some ways you can utilize the Bible to help you develop your spiritual life. All of these suggestions are very simple but will be helpful, if put into practice. Through the years the Bible has enriched my life and I have come to love it. I hope you will love and cherish its teachings also, if you do not already.

TAKE TIME

First, develop a time to study the Bible systematically and regularly. You need to set aside a particular time each day — whether it is morning or night — and use that time to read the Scriptures. Please don't go hop-skipping through the Bible or use the hunt and peck approach as your method of reading the Scriptures. That can be a very dangerous approach. Suppose your finger happens to land on the verse for the day, "And Judas went out and hanged himself." That's not a very good motto for the day, is it? Well, you don't like that one, so you go searching for another one. "Go thou and do likewise" is the next one you flip over to. Develop a regular habit of reading the Bible and don't go skipping all through its pages.

READ ONE BOOK AT A TIME

Secondly, learn to read one book of the Bible at a time. Select a book, like the Gospel of Mark, if you have not done much reading of the Scriptures, and begin with it. Read the Gospel of Mark by beginning at the beginning and read through it in its entirety. Begin the Book of the Psalms by starting with the first Psalm and continue reading through the book until you finish it. Read at least a chapter a day. Meditate and reflect thoughtfully upon the passage. When you hop all around the Bible, you will not be able to understand its message much at all.

Suppose I was separated from my wife on a trip overseas. Suppose I wrote her a love letter filled with my love and devotion to her. Before I mailed that letter to her, I sat down and cut out certain sections and decided to keep them for myself. I then mailed the fragments to her. What would it mean to her? Oh, she might make some sense of lines or phrases in one place or another. But it would be so confusing and disjointed that she couldn't put my thoughts together very well and understand what I was trying to tell her.

The same result would be true in music, if you tried to play a song with only fragments of the music. It would not make sense, and you could not understand it. If you cut pages at random out of a novel by Ernest Hemingway, you couldn't make any sense out of the story. You would not understand his plot at all. Too often that is the way we read the Bible. And, then, we wonder why it doesn't make much sense to us. I encourage you to read the Bible a book at the time. Spend time with each book. Move through it slowly.

USE MANY TRANSLATIONS

Thirdly, use various translations as you read the Bible. The King James Version was translated and put on the market in 1611. That is a long time ago now. The manuscripts which scholars used for that version of the Bible came from the tenth century. New Testament scholars have discovered over five thousand errors in these manuscripts which those who copied them made. In 1948 the Dead Sea Scrolls were discovered. These manuscripts were written in the first and second century. They are nine centuries older than the ones used by the King James Version. Some of the newer translations are far better, because they rely on these earlier manuscripts.

The King James Version is beautiful, but some of its words have a different meaning today. In one place a writer noted that David "prevented" the dawning of the morning. That is a pretty good act, even for David. But "prevent" in the English usage of that day meant "to come before." In another place the King James Version reads that we should be holy in our "conversation." Well, we should be, but the word "conversation" in that day didn't mean speaking — it meant "walking."

Select a translation that you can understand. Translations like Good News for Modern Man, Williams, The New English Bible, the International Version, the Contemporary Version, or The New Revised Standard Version are all translations that are written in today's language and are based on older manuscripts. Many people have difficulty with the King James Version today because much of it is written in a language we don't use any more. No one says, "Thee," "thou," "thine," "art," "whence," and other such words. Most cannot understand them today. Select a translation for your Bible study that is readable.

USE RESOURCES

Fourthly, use available resources to help you to understand the Bible. When I was teaching at the Seminary, a student told me that all he thought he needed to preach was the Bible. "Then you are going to have some poor preaching," I responded. We all need to have some help in understanding the Scriptures. If you really want to be serious about your Bible study, I would suggest that you invest in some good commentaries or use copies from the church library. *The Interpreter's One-Volume Commentary on the Bible, Harper's Bible Commentary* (1988), or Peake's *Commentary of the Bible* are excellent one volume commentaries.

William Barclay's New Testament commentaries, and the *Daily Study Bible Series* (Westminster Press) for the Old Testament which was developed in Scotland and England are older resources but very useful. *The Layman's Bible Commentary* by John Knox Press or *The Layman's Bible Book Commentary* by Broadman Press are also older but still good resources. If you are willing to invest more money, or can get them from your church library, you may want to consult *The New Interpreter's Bible*, (Abingdon Press) *the Interpretation* commentaries (John Knox Press), or *Smyth & Helwys* commentaries. These scholars can help you understand the background of the passage and the nature of the material you are studying. These resources can be very helpful in your understanding the Bible better.

In the story recorded in the passage of Scripture from Acts eight (Acts 8:26-36), the Ethiopian eunuch asked: "How can I understand what I am reading without some help?" How can any of us really understand the Bible without getting some help? Consult good biblical resources; use commentaries; and be willing to talk to someone else who has spent his or her life studying the Scriptures so you can learn from them.

GET THE CONTEXT

Fifth, as you read a book of the Bible, be sure first of all, to set it within the context of its own day. We often move too quickly to try to discover the message it may have for our day before we have understood what its message was for the ancient world for which it was written in the first place. That is the reason we have so many strange interpretations about Revelation and Daniel. These interpreters have often not been willing to see why the writer wrote the book in the first place. Ask questions like, "What kind of literature is it?" "Is it prose, poetry, a parable, proverb, a letter, or a song?" They are all understood in different ways. "To whom was it written?" "Why was it written?" "Was this Old Testament book written by somebody from Babylon back to family or friends in Jerusalem?" "Was it written by the Apostle Paul from a city like Ephesus to another church?" Ask the question — who, when, where, why, how, to whom? When you know its original, natural meaning, you will be able to interpret it better for our own day.

MEMORIZE SOME SCRIPTURE

In the sixth place, I would also encourage you to memorize some of the Scripture you read each day. As you read your particular passage for the day, why not select a key verse or two to keep with you for the whole day? If you are reading where Jesus says, "I have come that you might have life and have it more abundantly," think what a marvelous passage that could be to strengthen you throughout the day. "I can do all things through Christ who strengthens me" is another powerful verse to store in our mind. In trials and tribulations think what that verse can mean. "Thy word have I hid in my heart," the psalmist said. When we have hidden Scripture in our heart, in times of need these verses can become a lamp to our feet and a light to our pathway.

Memorizing Scripture enables you to have the Bible with you always. The texts are stored in your mind to sustain you whenever you need them. In times of grief, pain, depression, and difficulties you can draw upon the Scriptures within your own mind, because you have spent years memorizing them.

During the Korean conflict, my first cousin was an oceanographer on the Pueblo. He was one of the two civilians who was imprisoned when the Pueblo was captured by the Koreans. Everyone on board the Pueblo spent many months in prison. The prisoners were not allowed to have reading material of any kind — the Bible included. Richard had been brought up in church and had attended faithfully as a child and teenager. He had memorized many passages of Scripture. The men longed desperately for some inspiration. He would write verses of Scripture on toilet tissue and then, during their time in the exercise yard, he would pass the piece of paper to one of them. He, in turn, would read it and pass it on to another. The words from the Bible brought them strength during a difficult time, because one man had taken time to memorize them earlier in his life. You can't do that if you have never memorized any Scripture. That practice can make the Scriptures a continuous part of your heart and mind.

KEEP A JOURNAL

Seven. I would also encourage you in the seventh place, to keep a journal as you read the Scriptures. Jot down any thoughts or ideas that leap into your mind as you read the Bible. Make a record of what book of the Bible you are reading, what helps you are using, and the inspiration, hope, or guidance it provides you for the day. This will only take a few moments, but it can be very beneficial to you.

READ WITH EXPECTANCY

Eight, I hope you will also read the Scriptures with an open mind, expecting God's spirit to breathe his fresh creativity upon you. Don't read it hurriedly like the morning newspaper. Read reflectively, awaiting further light from God as you journey into new territory of the Bible. Too often we approach the Bible assuming already that we know what the passage means. We need to open our minds so God's spirit can guide us into new insights an in new directions.

Earlier in his life Luther had difficulty in understanding the righteousness of God. He had come to despise it. One day, as he was reading again Romans 1:17, "For in it the righteousness of God is revealed through faith for faith; as it is written, 'He who through faith is righteous shall live,'" he received fresh insight into a passage he had read hundreds of times.

At this point I felt completely reborn, and as if I had entered paradise with its open gate. In a moment the whole meaning of Scripture seemed to have changed. Thereafter I ran through the Scriptures as if I had them in my memory, and collected analogical meanings in other words, such as the word of God, which means the work that God works in us, the virtue of God, which means the virtue through which he makes us powerful, the wisdom of God, which means the wisdom through which he makes us wise, the courage of God, the salvation of God, the glory of God. My love for that sweetest word righteousness of God was henceforth as great as my hatred for it had been hitherto. In this way, this passage of Paul was truly the gate of Paradise.[79]

It is hard to imagine what paths God could take us down, if we would be open and receptive to him. Our own narrowness and assumed knowledge often blocks his efforts to guide us. Let's stop assuming that we already know what the Bible is saying and "listen" attentively to God.

READ WITH IMAGINATION

I would also encourage you in the ninth place, to read the Scriptures with imagination. I am not encouraging you to take some wild fantasy, but to try and put yourself back into that Scripture setting. If you are reading, for example, the passage where blind Bartimaeus cries: "Lord, have mercy upon me." Try to see the crowd of people as they are walking by him as they are following Jesus and listening to his teaching. See if you can envision what Bartimaeus was like. See the mob around him, pushing him back, and trying to keep him in his place. See the desperation in his face, feel his panic. Try to imagine also his sense of expectation and hope as he hears Jesus drawing near. Try to picture the scene in your mind. Try also to see that you, like Bartimaeus are blind,

---

79   Luther, Martin, quoted in Roland Bainton, *Here I Stand* (New York: Abingdon, 1950), 65.

and need to see. You are also crying out for Jesus to help you "see." Try to see yourself within the setting so the story can address you.

Picture the setting where Moses was on a wilderness mountainside tending sheep. Try to depict the barrenness of that place. See the sheep as they are feeding nearby. In your mind's eye you may picture Moses resting as he leans against a rock. Suddenly a bush begins to burn on the mountainside. Imagine the fear, awe, and wonder that overtakes him.

Picture in your mind another occasion where a man is traveling down a road, and suddenly robbers attack him. See the place where it happens. Notice its isolation, his fear and panic. Imagine that you are that person. See if you can get inside the story so that you can see it in a different way. Are you the man who is attacked? Are you one of the robbers or the good Samaritan?

Let your imagination take you into the Upper Room, at the trial of Jesus, His crucifixion, at Pentecost, along with Paul on one of his missionary journey's, or with an Old Testament prophet or traveling with Jesus and listening to His teachings. Let the passage become real for you.

LET THE BIBLE READ YOU

Finally, when you read the Scriptures, remember most of all that they need to read you. The Word of God comes into your life and judges you. It lifts a mirror in front of you. It brings God's spirit before us to address our lives and show us how far removed we are from his way, the goal to which he has beckoned us to move toward, and the kind of life he want us to live. See the mirror in the Bible which is lifted up for us to see our image. As Soren Kierkegaard has said the Scriptures are "a letter from God with your personal address on it." See your name written in the Bible. God is speaking to you through the Bible. "Just as you do not analyze the words of someone you love, but accept them as they are said to you," Dietrich Bonhoeffer wrote, "accept the Word of Scripture and ponder it in your heart, as Mary did. That is all. That is meditation."[80]

The assurance of the writer of the 23rd Psalm becomes a word of encouragement to you. The doubt of Thomas reflects your own struggle with faith. The denial of Peter reminds you of your own weakness. The disciples' request of Jesus to teach them how to pray becomes your own plea. The Bible is a timeless book. It speaks out of the life of a people from the past to speak to you today.

The Bible does not separate religion from life. Religion infuses all of life. The Bible reminds us that God searches our thoughts and knows our ways. Religion is not a subject which you can simply select or discard as you please. Genuine religion touches your life every day and requires daily commitment. "I'm not so much concerned about the part of the Bible that I don't understand," Mark Twain once said, "as those parts I *do* understand." What we understand of the Bible, without question, is sufficient to guide us into the abundant life. As we travel the journey of life, the Bible throws the light from its guiding beam to show us the pathway. Through his written Word, God's judgment, forgiveness, redemption, and everlasting life are made known.

During the Second World War, a chaplain was sailing on a ship with fifteen hundred Marines who were being brought back to the United States from Japan to be discharged. He received a request from some of them to have a Bible study each morning. He was surprised by their request but quickly told them that he would be glad to do it. Each morning he met with the Marines for a time of Bible study. One day they studied the passage about the raising of Lazarus from the dead. The chaplain interpreted this passage as the fulfillment of Jesus' words, "I am the resurrection and the life. If any man believes in me he will not die." Trying to drive home his point, he drew upon Dostoevsky's famous novel *Crime and Punishment*. He told them the story of Raskolnikov who had destroyed

---

80   Bonhoeffer, Dietrich. *The Way to Freedom* (New York: Harper & Row, 1966), 59.

himself when he murdered another man. He was brought back to life through the reading of these words of Jesus.

After the Bible study was finished, he didn't think any great impact had been made on the men. As he was walking away from the group, one of the young soldiers walked with him and finally after struggling for a while said: "Chaplain, I felt as though everything we read this morning was pointed right at me. I've been living in hell for the last six months, and for the first time I feel as though I'd gotten free." He told his story about how he had gotten in real trouble while he was in occupied Japan. No one knew it but him, but his sense of guilt had been so severe that he did not think that he could face his family back home.

But that day in the Bible study his life was changed. "Until today, Chaplain," he said, "I've been a dead man. I have felt utterly condemned by myself, by my family (if they knew), and by God. *I've been dead*, but now, after reading about Jesus and Lazarus, I know that I am alive again. The forgiveness of God can reach out even to me. The resurrection Jesus was talking about is a real thing, after all, right now."

That Word comes to us from the Scriptures that we can become a new person in Jesus Christ. Read the Scriptures with the awareness that they meet you and communicate the Word of God to you. Be open and responsive to that Word. It is a well from which you can draw water for all of your life. It is an inexhaustible source that you can never use up. Let it nourish your life. Feed upon it every day and let it help sustain you.

CHAPTER II

WHERE IS GOD WHEN DEVASTATION AND SUFFERING REIGN?

Voices are often raised in times of suffering and tragedies that seek to carry us down a path away from the assurance of God's presence. When some Christian people hear about what happened in a devastating earthquake in Haiti or some other part of the world, they quickly ask: "Why did God let this happen?" That is the question of many from seven to seventy. "Where was God when this happened? Why didn't God prevent it?" Some shout that these kinds of episodes prove there is no God. Pain, suffering, and death raise their voices in agonizing screams. I have no simple or glib answer to this dilemma. I agree with Phillips Brooks who said that he would shut his ears to anyone who claimed to be able to explain the mystery of suffering and evil. But I would like to offer for your consideration some thoughts that might help us sort through this problem and find footing on the pathway of faith as we listen for the "voice" of God on our journey through this dark valley.

A VALID CONCEPT OF GOD

I think we need to begin with a valid concept of God. I do not believe for a second that the good God we worship deliberately sent the earthquake to kill innocent people in Haiti. Pat Robertson on "The 700 Club," following that event, said that the earthquake occurred because of a curse the Haitians had made with the Devil to get free from the French several hundred years ago. What kind of God does this depict? A god who would send an earthquake to kill innocent people, in my opinion, would be demonic. That kind of god would be my Devil! These shameful comments by Robertson voice the same kind of views that the Terrorists claim about God. This is a distorted and inadequate concept of God. "I have learned the inadequacy of facile and absolute answers in the midst of complexity and ambiguity," Paul Simmons, clinical professor of medical ethics at the University of Louisville, observed. "I also have learned the indispensability of biblical wisdom for the comfort and guidance it provided to those familiar with its pages and open to its counsel. I recoiled at stories of human tragedy and encounters with the great issues of life. The challenge is always to study the Scriptures to 'rightly discern' wisdom and truth."[81]

Our understanding of God is revealed in the life and teachings of Jesus Christ. What kind of God would we worship if God saw a healthy teenager and said, "I am going to break his leg because he has committed a bad deed recently?" How could we serve a God who saw a young mother and said, "I'm going to take the life of her child so she will worship me?" This is the same logic of Robertson's view of God. As we reflect on the awful earthquake, do not lay the blame on God or call it the "will of God." I cannot believe nor comprehend any view of a good God who would condone such a horrific act. Jesus has taught us that God is like a loving father who is filled with compassion, concern, forgiveness and grace. The first step in sorting out this problem is remembering the kind of God we worship.

Nicholas Wolterstorff, in writing about his response to the death of his son in a mountain climbing accident, acknowledges that "To the 'why' of suffering, we get no firm answer. Of course some sufferings are easily seen to be the result of our sin: war, assault, poverty, amidst plenty, the hurtful wind. And maybe some in chastisement. But not all. The meaning of the remainder is not told us. It eludes us. Our net of meaning is too small."[82] We search for answers. But none comes easily. We must do as Wolterstorff did,

81 Simmons, Paul D. *Faith and Health: Religion, Science, and Public Policy* (Macon, GA: Mercer University Press, 2008), 16.
82 Wolterstorff, Nicholas. *Lament for a Son* (Grand Rapids, Michigan: William B. Eerdmans Publishing Co., 1987), 74.

step out in the darkness of grief, suffering and lack of certain knowledge in faith in the God we have seen in Jesus Christ. "Faith is a footbridge that you don't know will hold you up over the chasm," he asserts, "until you're forced to walk out onto it."[83]

A VALID VIEW OF EVIL

We also need a valid view of sin and evil. Our English language is limited in describing evil. We use the same word to depict natural evil and human evil. Natural evil comes about through the destruction caused by earthquakes, floods, hurricanes, fires, tornados and the like. We cannot control nature, and we know that it rains on "the just and the unjust." Another step that might shed some light on the problem of understanding natural evil and suffering is an awareness of the kind of world in which we live. God has created a world in which natural laws are operating. If that were not the case, nothing in life would be dependable. We can sit on a pew in church and know that it is not going to change into a wild animal because of the dependability of natural laws. When you leave church and turn the key in your car, you know that your car will not be transformed into a bowl of jelly because of the laws of nature. I taught my children not to play with matches; not to run in the street in front of a car and not to touch a hot fire so they could understand the importance and consequences of the natural laws of our world. If I jump off a ten-story building, I can't change my mind halfway down. The law of gravity will be enforced.

If an airplane is flown into a building, like the terrorists did on 9/11, it will crash and explode. That is a law of nature. The laws of our universe are not put aside because someone uses a good thing for an evil end. We have learned to fly by understanding certain natural laws. Airplanes can be used to transport people, bomb a military base or take the lives of innocent people by crashing into a building. The laws of nature are not evil but evil persons can use the natural laws for evil ends.

---

83   Ibid., 76.

I confess that I do not understand why nature itself can seem so evil sometimes. The devastation from tornados, earthquakes, floods or hurricanes indicates that God has given the natural world some freedom as it follows the natural laws of the universe. When God looked on creation, God said that it was "very good" — not perfect or complete (See Genesis 1:31). Maybe that is what Paul meant when he wrote that "the creation itself will be set free from its bondage." (Romans 8:21). I do not know why we have cancer, AIDS, TB or certain insects like the mosquito. We do not go against God's will when we try to eradicate them. If they have a beneficial function, I do not know what it is. I can also assure you if a mosquito lands on my arm, I will swat it and not think I am going against God's will. Although we do not fully understand all about nature or the laws of nature, nevertheless, we know enough to live as best we can in cooperation with these laws.

A VALID UNDERSTANDING OF GOD'S POWER

We describe God as omnipotent or all-powerful. If God is all-powerful, why doesn't God prevent horrible events, like the destruction of earthquakes similar to the one in Haiti or floods that destroy hundreds of homes and often take many lives, from happening? I believe that God has limited God's power by endowing nature with freedom and giving human beings freedom and choice. If we did not have freedom to make choices, then we would be robots. By putting "limits" on God's power, God allows us the freedom to make choices. God wants us to choose good, but God will give us the freedom to choose evil. Without this freedom, we could not grow as authentic persons. Without the possibility of choosing evil, there could be no possibility of good; there cannot be a possibility of being brave, I believe, without the possibility of being a coward; there cannot be the possibility of loving without the possibility of being unloving. Life is filled with choices: evil or good, faith or doubt, hope or despair, love or hate, etc.

God gives us freedom to choose where we live. Unfortunately, some people choose to live where earthquakes, floods, hurricanes, etc. happen. The choice was their own and not God's. Every person in God's world is a free, moral individual to make his or her own decision. God wants us to make good choices and not sinful ones. But God gives us the freedom to decide.

Some have said that if we pray right, God will spare Christians from suffering and evil. I have been a minister a long time and I can tell you pointedly that this is not true. I have known some of the finest Christians one could mention who have experienced accidents, pain, suffering, cancer, heart attacks, accidents, grief and death. You and I both know that many of those who have perished in earthquakes and floods were probably fine Christians. I have heard ministers who lived in the area of the Haitian earthquake testify to the deep faith of many of the Haitian people. I do not believe for a second that God was smiting these people with an earthquake to punish them or to send a message to the rest of the world.

WHERE WAS GOD?

Where was God when this devastating event occurred? God was right there suffering with the people in the earthquake as God did when Jesus was suffering and dying on the cross. God's Presence was surrounding those persons in the last moments of their lives in this world with the divine arms of love. God could never have been closer to them than God was in their moments of dying. God was assuring them that not even this horrible death would separate them from God's love, grace and presence. That's the Apostle Paul's great cry in Romans 8:38-39 "Nothing in all the universe can separate us from God's presence." Nothing! But most of all remember that, although we may not have the answer to the problem of evil and suffering, we have the *Presence* of the Eternal God with us no matter what happens and nothing; nothing can ever separate us from that Presence.

SOME WAYS TO RESPOND

In the light of suffering and difficulties that are a part of life, how should we respond to the needs of the Haitians and others like them who suffer and to our own needs and perspectives? Let me make a few concrete suggestions as we walk through this valley filled with "shadows."

Pray

First, pray for the Haitians or any who suffer from devastations of any kind. Pray for those who have lost loved ones that God may bring them comfort. Pray for those who have suffered, hunger and thirst and lost their homes and possessions. Pray for our Baptist mission workers and those from other religious groups who are offering aid and assistance. Pray for the medical workers, the Red Cross, the volunteers, governmental support from around the world, and all those who are trying to render assistance and help in the rebuilding of this country. Pray for anyone when they are ill, suffering, perplexed, grieving, facing dearth, or struggling with some other devastating dilemma.

Give

Second, give financially to assist the need. You can give through the special offering by various denominational mission boards. Or through the special offering that church youth groups have in a program called 30 Hours of Fasting, or through mission groups in your church. You can join these special fast programs or simply give as you are led.

Go

Third, Go. You may have an opportunity to go under the supervision of various mission boards and volunteer to help in construction, offer assistance in supplying medical aid, food, water, clothes or some other needy area. Closer at hand, you can visit a friend or relative, who has experienced an illness, grief or some other difficult time, and be an encourager and supporter.

Not the Will of God

Fourth, remember that this earthquake or other natural disasters are not "The Will of God," nor should you believe that God sent this earthquake or other difficulties to punish them or teach us a lesson. God has given nature freedom just as God has given freedom to human beings

Nature is free. Nature has freedom to develop and function. God didn't send the earthquake. It is just part of the natural order. Christians, like you and I, are not spared from its destructive force. Many wonderful Christians suffered from this earthquake. Natural events like this one are a result of the freedom which God has given the universe and not a sign of God's anger or a desire to punish someone for their sins.

Equip Yourself for the Unexpected

That thought leads me to the next suggestion. We've got to learn how to live with difficulties. Many of us have a hard time learning to live with earthquakes, snow storms, floods, other disasters, disadvantages, and difficulties. We want everything always to be nice, easy and smooth. We cannot always control what happens to us, but we can control how we respond.

Peppermint Patty, one of the characters in the Peanuts comic strip, called Charlie Brown and said, "Chuck, its disaster time. I am supposed to read a book over the Christmas holidays. What do I do?"

"You mean you want me to suggest a book?" he asked.

"No! No! No! How do I get out of it? How do I avoid it?"

Now, that's what most of us want to do when disasters and difficulties come. How can I escape this? How can I get away from it?

But we don't always. Disasters and difficulties are a part of life. They come to the good and to the bad and to the saints and to the sinners. We all receive sunshine and rain. We don't escape them. We have to learn to see the constructive that comes from the destructive. Difficulties may become doorways to growth and progress.

I read about a baby who was born that did not cry when it was first born. Later, when they were putting diapers on the baby, (this was when they still used pins that would stick) they noticed there was no sense of pain when the baby was stuck with a pin. The doctors advised the parents that the child would be in great danger through life because she did not have a system that would respond to pain. We sometimes say, "Oh, wouldn't it be wonderful if I never had any problems, difficulties or burdens." But if you and I were insensitive to these experiences we would soon learn that life would be far worse than we could ever imagine. You and I have to learn that we learn from difficulties. We must learn the advantages of disadvantages.

Advantages out of Disadvantages

Six, leads me to this: Some of the most important and significant accomplishments that have ever come about in society have come about from persons who have experienced great difficulties. The list could be almost endless of musicians, poets, inventors and others who have discovered new inventions, or written music, poetry or books or accomplished other worthy things in the midst of disasters. One of our greatest musicians, Frederick Chopin, suffered a great deal during his life. But he wrote some of the most beautiful music during this time. Alexander Pope was greatly deformed and was considered so ugly by some people that they couldn't stand to be near him. But he wrote some of the most beautiful poetry imaginable. Dostoevsky, the Russian novelist, was an epileptic. Yet from his pen came some of the greatest novels that we have ever experienced. Some of the greatest inventions have come during times of war, or during times of disasters. Many people have learned to be creative and grow during such times. I believe that our character is forged out of learning how to bring the best out of the worst, advantages out of disadvantages, and by making the best of the worst kind of situation. Maybe a much more constructive, secure, stable and productive nation in Haiti will arise from its rubble and destruction after it is rebuilt.

Expect the Unexpected

Seven, go a step further. I think, also, we've got to learn to expect the unexpected. There are so many people who go through life and they never think anything is supposed to happen that is going to create a problem for them. And, when the unexpected comes, they panic. But we must learn to expect the unexpected. The unexpected is simply a part of life. Sometimes snowstorms come. Sometimes earthquakes, floods, and hurricanes come. Sometimes heavy rains come. Sometimes we may go a long time without rain. Sometimes there is illness or difficulties.

Some people have difficulty with difficulties simply because they have not learned to equip themselves for the unexpected. The unexpected is often a part of our lives. Hurricanes, blizzards, tornadoes, earthquakes, floods, and other natural disasters are simply a part of life. How we respond to them, when we are in their pathway, will often determine what kind of life we will really have.

God has given nature freedom just as God has given human beings freedom to continue to develop, grow and improve. I don't believe that God sends these kinds of storms upon us. They are a part of the natural universe that God has created and nature is still in the process of developing. God said that the creation was "very good" – not perfect.

When we have learned to expect the unexpected, we will build within ourselves resources to combat them. There are some people who do not have strength to draw upon during this time, because they have not fortified themselves ahead of time. I am not surprised, when a person who has no experience with God, who never darkens the doors of a church, who has never worked to develop his or her spiritual life, is shaken to the core when some catastrophic event comes. They have not done anything to fortify and equip themselves within to be prepared for the unexpected. When we have laid spiritual foundations, and fortified the inner person, then we can learn to withstand the storms that come no matter how serious they are or no matter how unexpected or vile they may be. We have the inner assurance that God is there with us.

John Baillie, the late Scottish theologian, has summoned us to pray the following way when we encounter various circumstances in life:

> *Let me use disappointment as material for patience;*
> *Let me use success as material for thankfulness;*
> *Let me use anxiety as material for perseverance;*
> *Let me use danger as material for courage;*
> *Let me use criticism as material for learning;*
> *Let me use praise as material for humility;*
> *Let me use pleasure as material for self-control;*
> *Let me use pain as material for endurance.*[84]

MATERIAL POSSESSIONS ARE NOT THE MOST IMPORTANT THING

Eight, and then we may also learn that material possessions are not the most important things in life. As important as houses and property may be, they are not the most important things in your life and my life. People are. Spiritual values are. We need to nurture these values, because sooner or later every single one of us will lay down whatever material possessions he or she has and pass through the portals into the spiritual dimension to be with God. Then the big question is, "What are you taking with you?" If all our material possessions are gone and we have deep, abiding spiritual

---

84 Baillie, John. *A Diary of Private Prayer*, Updated and Revised by Suzanne Wright (New York: Scribner, 2014), 95.

values, then we still have the most lasting values of all. Spiritual and moral values are the most important. In conversation with Douglas Abrams, Archbishop Desmond Tutu reminds us that "discovering more joy does not, I'm sorry to say, save us from the inevitability of hardship and heartbreak. In fact, we may cry more easily, but we will laugh more easily. Perhaps we are just more alive." Continuing, he observed: "Yet as we discover more joy, we can face suffering in a way that ennobles rather than embitters. We have hardship without becoming hard. We have heartbreak without being broken." "The ultimate source of happiness is within us," he affirms. "Not money, not power, not status.... We must look inside."[85]

In All Things Give Thanks

Nine: In writing to the Thessalonians, as recorded in the fifth chapter, the eighteenth verse, Paul admonished, "In all things give thanks to God." Paul *didn't say* give thanks *for all* things but *in* all things. Thanksgiving is not reserved just for the good times. Paul urged his readers to learn the difficult lesson of expressing thanksgiving in the midst of the bad times as well as in the good times. A vital faith makes us want to lift our voices in praise: "Now thank we all our God." We need to learn to praise God on rainy days as well as on bright sunny days. We need to learn to praise God on dark days as well as on bright days. We need to learn to praise God in days of discouragement as well as in times when we are on the mountaintops filled with enthusiasm. We need to express praise to God in times of illness as well as in times of health. We need to learn to express thanksgiving to God in times of death as well as in times of life. We exclaim with Job: "The Lord gives and the Lord takes away. Blessed be the name of the Lord" (Job 1:21)

A small book has an interesting title: *The Choice is Always Ours.* It is an anthology of religious writings built around the theme that in every situation in life persons can make a choice. The writers acknowledge that we cannot always control what happens to us

85 Dalai Lama, Desmond Tutu, and Douglas Abrams, *The Book of Joy* (New York: Penguin Random House, 2016), 12, 14.

but we can control our response to the situation. Our response can make a difference. Do we give in, give up, panic, quit or see what other possibilities there might be? Learning to be grateful can be a meaningful choice in many situations.

We can learn to verbalize praise in all things when we know that nothing can separate us from the presence of God. Whether times are good or bad, God is still present with us to sustain us in everything that happens. Israel learned some of its greatest lessons about God in the wilderness. Paul had suffered greatly for God through persecution, imprisonment, and rejection. But during all his suffering, he could still say, "In all things, give thanks unto God."

GOD IS EVER PRESENT

Ten, and last, I would mention this. During an earthquake or any disaster, we still have the assurance that this event, as devastating as it was, has not blown away the presence of God. It has not taken God away from us. Job reminds us (Job 38:22-30) that God created all the universe, and ultimately God is the source of all things. Remember the freedom that God has given nature. In the midst of God's natural order, which exercises its freedom or human beings their freedom, God is present with us. During your pain, suffering, agony or whatever, God is there. God is present. You can have the assurance that no matter how difficult life might be, God is closer than breath itself. Archbishop Desmond Tutu reminds us that "the path to joy, like sadness, did not lead away from suffering and adversity but through it... Nothing beautiful comes without some suffering."[86] But God is always with us — in the good and bad times, and always teaching us.

I love the story about the young man who was hired to work on a farm. The farmer thought this lad didn't seem too intelligent, because when the farmer asked him about certain matters, he got the same response. "I can sleep well on a windy night." When

---

86   Ibid., 150.

one of the fierce storms of the season came, the farmer leaped out of bed and went to wake the lad. He couldn't wake him. The lad was sleeping through the storm. The farmer ran out to check for damage, but discovered the barn doors were securely shut. The hay was fastened down. Every place he went, everything was secure. Then he realized what that young lad had meant. "I can sleep well on a windy night." He slept well because he had prepared himself for the storm.

When we have snowstorms or earthquakes, or other disasters, they may destroy lots of things, even when they are fastened down. But we can still rest secure when we know that we are anchored in God. We know that nothing can remove the power of God's presence in our life. Let us remember no matter how angry a storm, earthquake or difficulty may be, whether it is a personal and very private storm of your own struggle, or whether it is a public, community or national disaster, God is still with us to help us to learn, grow and develop. May you and I then learn, even from an angry earthquake or any disaster that we are not separated for God's Presence. Let us continue to believe even in the darkness and silence.

CHAPTER 12

ON NOT LOSING
YOUR VISION

In life, there are two basic ways of seeing. One is positive; the other is negative. One perspective sees only the darkness; the other is able to see the beginning of dawn. The one can see only defeat; the other is able to see victory. One is only able to see despondency; the other can see hope. One is able to see only a pile of rubble; another sees materials from which to begin rebuilding. One sees a dead-end street; another sees opportunity to make a new road. One person sees a glass, half-empty; the other sees it half-full. How do you see? Do you have negative or positive vision in life? Most of the time, when we talk with someone, we can tell rather quickly how they see, because they reveal almost immediately in their conversation whether they see life with negative eyes or positive vision.

NEGATIVE VISION

The two stories found in Numbers 13:25-33 and Matthew 17:14-20 speak about negative and positive vision. Let us look for a moment at these stories. Notice, first, that there, is a great deal of negative vision which they project toward life. The children of Israel, according to this Old Testament selection, had moved to the very edge of the Promised Land. They had traveled for forty years in the wilderness. Now Moses sent some spies to go into the land that lay before them to see what it was like. Twelve men, one from each tribe, traveled for forty days through the land, probably moving in the darkness of night, and scurrying about here and there in the daytime, trying not to be seen as they observed the land and the people who lived there. They discovered that, compared to the desert where they had been for forty years, this was a very fertile land. It was indeed flowing with milk and honey. Their report pictured the land as being fantastically rich with promise. To prove their point, they returned with pomegranates, figs, and a large bunch of grapes swinging on a long pole. The great luxury of the land could be seen by all.

Caleb was the spokesman. He declared: "Let us go up at once and occupy the country; we are well able to conquer it." Joshua sided with him, but the other ten were reluctant and exclaimed: "Wait a minute, these people look like giants to us. They are the sons of Anak, the 'long-necked' ones." Goliath, some scholars believe, may have been a descendant. These men looked gigantic to these former slaves. "We look like grasshoppers to them," they cried. Their attitude is astounding. God's presence had been with them through all of their years of wandering and now, as they get ready to enter the Promised Land, they take a tremendously negative view. Fear had overtaken them, and their enemy seemed like large giants. "We are grasshoppers," they said. Grasshoppers are helpless, feeble, and have a low perspective toward life.

A GRASSHOPPER VIEW OF LIFE

We all know something about the grasshopper view of life, don't we? Some of us, if we are older, can recall those days when we were very small and everybody did look like giants to us. Remember the days in elementary school when you looked up at all of the giants around you, until you yourself began to grow up and you became a giant to someone else. It is amazing how often in life we see whatever obstacles arise before us as giants to be conquered. We feel as insignificant as grasshoppers, and a negative view slowly begins to permeate everything we do in our reaction to life. Instead of the highest goal possible, we reach toward the lowest maximum we can achieve as we seek to make our contribution in life. With this negative view toward life, we try to get by with the very least that we can. We often do this in our marriage. We do it in our church life and in our business life. We take this approach in almost every area of our life. We aim at the lowest common denominator and live out this negative view toward life. We become satisfied with the least we can do and do not reach for the highest within us.

Professors and teachers in school detect this perspective from students rather quickly. When they assign a paper to students, hands go up and the student asks: "Does it have to be ten pages? Can it be less?" Many students would not dream of writing a paper longer than the minimum page. "Does it have to have a bibliography?" "Does it need footnotes?" Most want everything else excluded so they can do the least amount of work required. Many do not have the desire to do the kind of research that will make them the best informed student they need to be, but seek, instead, the avenue which requires the least amount of effort. There is no excitement or enthusiasm for the subject. Too often that is the same approach we take toward our religion. It is often our approach toward marriage, parenting, and unfortunately, toward too much of life. The desire to get by with the least we can do is a negative attitude which is reflected often in our words and deeds.

Charlie Brown came walking out of his house to feed Snoopy one day. Snoopy was lying on top of his doghouse. Charlie Brown said to him, as he poured his dog food: "This food has been no trouble at all for me to fix for you today. It is just dry cereal and all I had to do was pour some water in it and it is ready to eat." Snoopy looked at it and, after Charlie Brown walked away, he said: "I'd rather be worth a little trouble." The things in life which are really worthwhile usually require a little trouble. But too often we give way to the negative view and not the positive and seek to do the least we can.

LOST THEIR VISION OF THE POWER OF GOD

Notice, also, in these stories that these people had lost their vision of the power of God. In some ways it is almost astounding that the children of Israel would have that happen to them when they had lived daily with God going before them as a pillar of fire. Through this pillar of fire, God's presence had been made known. Now as they are getting ready to go into the Promised Land, they have forgotten about this presence and now they see only the giants which loom before them and have forgotten about God.

LOOK BRIEFLY AT THE NEW TESTAMENT STORY.

The transfiguration has just taken place. Jesus has been transfigured before some of his disciples. Moses and Elijah appeared
there on the mountain with Jesus. When Jesus came back down from the
mountain following the transfiguration, He found a young lad who
was possessed by a demon. He discovered that His disciples were unable to cure the boy, and He said: "Oh you of little faith." Sometimes
we have lots of faith on the mountaintops of life, but, when we come down
into the valleys where there are difficulties and problems, our faith
seems to be inadequate to sustain us.

Raphael, in a marvelous painting of this scene, shows Jesus on the
mountaintop transfigured with Moses and Elijah. The disciples
with him are lying on the ground in an attitude of deepest awe.
Down in the valley below, one can see the other disciples surrounded
by a crowd of people, with the father and his young tormented
son whom the disciples are helpless to cure. Some are pointing up
toward the mountaintop where Christ is and where they will draw
their source of strength.

WHY DID THEY LOSE THEIR VISION?

Why do you suppose that the Israelites and the disciples responded in such a negative way?

They Were Afraid

Well, for one thing, they simply were afraid. The Israelites
saw the giants in the Promised Land, and they were fearful of
confronting them. The giants seemed too formidable to them. We,
too, know something of these kinds of fears when we seek to move forward
in life. We *see* individuals who are too threatening to us. Danger
seems to lurk at us from many sides. The obstacles appear too difficult,
so we fall back in great fear. We can't face the challenge. It seems
impossible. As young people, you have fears about college or what lies ahead
of you.

Years ago, I stood in the pulpit of a church that had a vision of a great building through which it might serve and minister in this community. They built that building and it has drawn people to use it and become members of the church. Some became discouraged soon by their debt, although the church was meeting it well. Others wondered if they would ever be able to build the children's building they need. Some became discouraged because the church had lost a few members to the church a former staff member started. They were afraid and wondered if they could possibility be the church they once were or could still be. During those years, it was amazing how some had lost their vision and slipped away and did not remain because fears of all kinds began to creep into their thinking. "Can we pay for it?" "Can we do this?" "Can we do the other?" Soon fear began to take over, instead of the vision which had guided them originally. But others saw the possibilities and trusted God and dared to move forward.

A Feeling of Helplessness

Notice that the Israelites and disciples had a feeling of helplessness. And so often do we. We, too, often have the grasshopper mentality. We think that the giants in the land are going to destroy us as we meet them. All kinds of giants loom before us, and we feel so helpless before their power. Some have become fearful, negative, cynical and pessimistic. What can we do against the might of the world powers when we seem so small and insignificant? We feel helpless because we forget the power of God. We think only about our own strength. We have forgotten the strength which we draw from God. The Israelites and the disciples alone needed to realize that by themselves they were helpless, but as they drew upon the strength and power of God, God enabled them to meet whatever force lay ahead of them. And so, can we.

Selfishness

Selfishness sometimes clouds our vision and causes us to lose sight of the power of God. We focus only upon our own needs. What I do is for my comfort. What I do is for my convenience. Our chief concern becomes what is good for me and makes me healthy and wealthy. Only what satisfies me becomes my chief emphasis. We soon forget about the concerns and needs of others in society and look only at ourselves. Church for some is basically what it can do for them. They ask: "What can I get from the church or out of it?" Will I be given what I want to make me happy and have a good time? There is no sense of a call to service or what I can do for Christ and his church.

A psychiatrist advised a woman one day to remove a mirror over her sink and to cut a window there. He said, "You wash your dishes every day, and all you ever do is look at yourself. You never get beyond your own immediate needs. You need to look through a window so you can see life in a wider perspective." Some of us never get beyond our own needs, and negativism takes over our perspective, because we see life only from our selfish needs and not from the wider angle of others in society being included in the picture.

Unbelief

A major reason that we lose a sense of the vision of God is because of unbelief. The Israelites began to see their faith grow weak as they thought about the giants before them. The disciples were not able to perform a miracle, Jesus said, because their faith was too weak. We know something about our own faith seeming to dissipate on occasions, don't we? Sometimes our own faith appears to disappear in the midst of crises, difficulties, and problems, because they seem overwhelming and we do not know where to turn.

In the small book, *Children's Letters to God,* one of the children wrote: "Dear Mr. God, how do you feel about people who don't believe in you? Somebody else wants to know. A friend, Neil." God, how do you feel about people who don't believe in you? Especially people who claim to believe in you? What do you think about people, God, when they get in the crises of life where they are experiencing suffering, pain, and difficulties and they find it hard to believe? When the whole world seems to be crashing around us, God, how do you feel about us?

God, of course, knows that we human beings are very weak. Before we are too hard on the Israelites, remember they had been slaves in Egypt and had wandered in that wilderness for forty years while they were searching, groping and hoping for the Promised Land. Sometimes our faith, like theirs, is too small.

THE SMALLEST FAITH IS TRANSFORMING

But notice the supreme lesson in these stories is this: Even the smallest amount of faith is transforming. The smallest amount of faith is transforming in the lives of individuals. Jesus said to his disciples: "If you have faith as a grain of mustard seed, you can remove mountains" (Matthew 13: 31-32). The mustard seed is a very tiny seed. The seeds look almost like pepper. They are so tiny. Jesus drew his image from the tiniest thing known to the people in that part of the world. "If you have the tiniest speck of faith," Jesus declared, "you have got possibilities of removing gigantic obstacles." Mountain was a Jewish metaphor for difficulty. The image was not to be taken literally. If you are going to sit down someplace one day and say, "I'll see if I've got enough faith to remove that mountain across the road from my house" then, you have missed the point of this image. For ancient Jewish people, a mountain was symbolic of great difficulties. If you have got the smallest amount of faith, you have the assurance that God will help you meet that difficulty.

I don't think we ever arrived in our pilgrim journey without questions and doubts. Like the disciple Thomas, we long to "see and touch" to believe. We travel by faith not sight or absolute certainty. We move forward searching for "the way, the truth, and the life" found in Christ. We travel with what Matthew Fox called "the disciplined pursuit of our holy curiosity." "We must pursue truth, work at it, sweat for it, just as we have to work at keeping our bodies healthy," Fox asserts. "The mind requires no less attention. The imagination can grow stale and flabby and weak if we do not seek out healthy food with which to nourish it."[87]

87   Fox, Matthew. *Creativity: Where the Divine and the Human Meet* (New York: Penguin Books, 2004). 76.

When I first began my pastorate in Bristol, Virginia, a young teenager named Steve Boyd came to see me one day. He came because his mother had made the appointment. Steve didn't like that very much. In fact, he told me later that it had made him mad. Steve's mother was upset with some of the religious and philosophical books that he was reading. She thought they might destroy his faith. He sat in my study, and we talked about his reading. I encouraged him to read and explore the faith. I assured him that our faith could withstand any kind of questions. And if it couldn't, it wouldn't be worth having. I assured him that the worse perspective was to assume we knew all the answers to the difficult questions in life. Some of the hard problems I put on a shelf awaiting further light.

Steve graduated at the head of his class at the University of Tennessee, went to Harvard Divinity School, and later received his doctor's degree from Harvard. Today he is teaching church history at Wake Forest University. When I was at Wake Forest University recently, Steve and I talked about the conversation we had several years ago in my study. He expressed appreciation to me for treating him as a person and giving him the freedom to think and raise questions.

I told him a story from my teen-age years. When I was about the same age that Steve had been when he talked with me, and had been a Christian only about a year, I went to my pastor with some questions I had about the scriptures. I didn't understand several texts. They seemed contradictory to me. His response was, "You are too young to be thinking about those things. You are just supposed to accept it." I never asked him another question! Because that was not my nature merely to accept something without thinking about it. I was a person who wanted to know why. "Explain it to me. I want to understand what it means," I asked. There is much of the disciple Thomas' nature within me. Nevertheless, like Thomas, I still pray: "Lord, I believe, help my unbelief." Step forward in faith, we must.

Now hear this. Faith has moved mountains in the past. Faith has removed kings. It has transformed empires. Faith has changed pagan culture. Faith has changed individuals. Faith has overcome mountains of greed, prejudice, selfishness, hostility, drunkenness, and laziness. Faith has removed all kinds of mountains in the past, and faith has also built churches, hospitals, universities, children's homes, and other creative agencies down through the centuries to help individuals live a better life. Faith has moved mountains, and faith has also built mountains of goodness in many places.

When we have even a small seed of faith, God begins to cut the giants down to size. If we live with the grasshopper approach to life, everything seems gigantic, but, when we have a small amount of faith, it begins to give us a new perspective on the giant difficulties which loom before us. We know we do not face them alone. We face our giants with the assurance of the power, presence and strength of God to enable us to meet them. "This is the victory that overcomes the world." The Scriptures say, "even our faith." Faith brings alive the power of Christ within us to enable us to face giants. Its transforming power, even as a speck, makes a great difference.

Although the disciples could not cure the young boy down in the valley below the mountain, later they were able to perform miracles in the name of Christ. As Peter and the other disciples went forth to minister, they did have healing powers through the presence of Christ. They did cure people. The same disciples, who did not have enough faith to heal before the resurrection, went forth after the resurrection with a great faith, and they transformed the world and turned it upside down in the name of Jesus Christ. You know that in your own life there have been instances in which you have felt the presence of God. You may have reached out with only a tiny speck of faith, and today you can affirm the difference it has made. "O Lord," the father said in the valley, "I believe, help thou my unbelief." And we make the same cry! Even a tiny bit of belief is sufficient to transform the mountains that are blocking our paths. Let's believe, so Christ can do his work through us.

We have all read stories about individuals who were caught in some traumatic situation. A father, for example, discovers his young son is trapped under a car and he reaches down and literally lifts the car off the child. The child is pulled out safely, and later the father tries to lift the car and he cannot budge it. How does that happen? Where does he get that strength? We don't know for sure. We are told by experts that individuals sometimes are able to get an enormous surge of hidden physical strength in *a* crisis, which they did not know they had. They draw upon latent strength to do an impossible feat in a sudden moment. These instances indicate the tremendous resources which we have within our body, mind, and spirit which are almost never tapped. How can we draw them forth from the hidden chambers of our inner life? Don't we wish we knew how we could do it? But isn't a part of what Christ is telling us here is that we begin to draw on this hidden power with a tiny seed of faith. That seed is the secret of bringing forth the powers within us.

When I walk with people during the crises of their lives, it is so tragic to witness those who have nothing to lean back upon, because they have made no preparation in good days to experience the power of God in their lives. They have no real experience of faith to sustain them. The tiny seed of faith could enable them to meet the great giants that will confront them along life's paths. Our faith can make the difference even if it is small.

OUR ATTITUDE AFFECTS US

When I have observed people during a crisis, the thing that I have learned, which has made all the difference to these persons, is their attitude — call it faith or vision. A person's attitude makes all the difference in the world in how individuals confront their crises. You may not be able to change the circumstances of your life, but your attitude can prevent the circumstances from changing you. That makes a radical difference. Sometimes the simplest task without a vision can seem an impossible drudgery. But when there is vision — a different attitude — the hardest task can be done with ease.

Before Lou Holtz went to coach at Notre Dame, he was coach for several years at the University of Minnesota. The team had a record of seventeen straight losses. They had lost every game by an average score of 47 to 13. Eighteen months later in 1985, Holtz took his team to the Independence Bowl. "It wasn't because of the coach," Holtz said. "It was because of their attitude."88 Whether it is football, work, or religion, one's attitude in a situation makes a radical difference. What is your attitude toward your problems and difficulties? Attitude is another way of speaking about vision.

THE IMPORTANCE OF VISION

It was vision that motivated Columbus to sail across an unknown ocean to search for a new world. It was vision that inspired Henry Ford to invent a horseless carriage. It was vision that animated Alexander Graham Bell to believe that persons could talk over a wire. It was vision that inspired the Wright Brothers to believe that human beings could fly. It was vision that heartened von Braun to believe that it was possible for men and women to go to the moon. It is vision that inspires poets and musicians, writers and artists, scientists and entrepreneurs, inventors and explorers, athletes and business persons. These people have a sense of call to something beyond what they are now. They have a pull, nudge, whisper, urge, drive, quest, longing, dissatisfaction or compulsion. There is something within that says there is more yet for them to be. They realize that they have not arrived.

What would religion be without vision? Abraham followed God's call in quest of a city without foundations. Moses followed God across a wilderness for forty years, believing that a promised land could become a reality. David had a vision of a united nation, and he brought to Israel the longest reign of peace that they ever experienced. Isaiah had a vision in the temple of God's presence high and lifted up. Jesus, our Lord, had a vision that the kingdom of God could be a reality. Paul had a vision that the gospel was

88 Hillkirk, John and Gary Jacobson, "Count On Me," *USA Weekend* (September 21-23, 1990).

not restricted to the Jewish people but was for persons of all races. Vision led David Livingston to go to Africa; Lottie Moon to go to China; Albert Schweitzer to go to Lambarene; Mother Teresa to go to India. Vision enables us to sense God's pull within us to be more than we have yet become or to serve in a special way.

The demands which come to us from Jesus about our faith seem to be unattainable. He has told us that we are supposed to love our enemies. Who among us really loves our enemies as we should? He instructed us "to do unto others as we would have them do unto us." Who among us does that completely? He commanded us to love our neighbors. Who among us really loves our neighbor fully? We have been challenged by Christ to be his servants in the world. Who among us is really totally serving or loving? Jesus has told us to "seek first the Kingdom of God and everything else will be added unto us." Who among us truly seeks first the Kingdom of God? Jesus has declared that we are to be perfect as our heavenly Father is. Who among is completely perfect?

These goals seem unattainable, and, yet, Jesus Christ has lifted them before us to challenge us as we follow him. We may begin with the smallest kind of faith, but we continue, then, to move toward the very highest that we can be, by God's grace and not the least, or the most unworthy. We are challenged to reach for the highest, the farthest, and for the greatest possibilities of what we can be. We may fall short, but we do not settle for the lowest goal we can achieve or a negative goal but for the highest, the best, and the most positive. He summons us to an extraordinary vision.

Michelangelo had a famous student, whom we have already eluded to earlier, whose name was Raphael. One day Michelangelo came to see some of the paintings of Raphael, and noticed a painting on an easel in which all the figures on it seemed to be so small, faint, and indistinguishable. Michelangelo took a brush and wrote across the painting, "Amplius! Larger!" He wanted the younger artist to know that if he were going to paint pictures, he had to quit trying to paint everything in its smallest perspective, but to *see* people, trees, and all of life in its largest possibilities. Our perspective of what God wants for us to be as individuals or as a church is usually too small. Young people and adults, as you step into the future, do not dream small dreams but large ones. God is calling us to do great things in God's name. Don't settle for a small dream.

Can you remember when your faith was warm, radiant, and vital? Your faith was real and your heart beat with joy. God seemed near and God's presence warmed your soul. For some of you, that faith has now grown cold, dull and damp. You no longer see the sunset of God's radiant presence beckoning you toward the horizons of the possibilities which life before you. I want to encourage you to let God's Spirit blow the breath of God's presence upon the coals of your faith, which have become cold, and let God fan them once again into a burning, radiant fire of affection. Let your faith come alive again by the warmth of God's presence. Celebrate the wonderful possibilities before the church today. Celebrate and be grateful for the outstanding and dedicated ministers, support staff, and laity who feel led to serve Christ in our world today. Celebrate the wonderful Sunday worship and Bible study times and the weekday studies in many of our churches. If these have grown tired or pale, strive to invigorate them with new insights and more inclusive and loving perspectives. Celebrate the Advent and Christmas services that enliven the church each year.

Despite all its weaknesses and flaws, I still believe that the church has a bright future before it, and is rich with new possibilities, challenges and ministries. Celebrate that! Affirm that! Recapture the vision when God first called you into faith. Your renewed vision does not have to be clothed in the same old garments of dogmatism, exclusive religion, or unChrist-like concepts of God or our mission in Christ's service. With renewed vision, you can see the possibilities you have for God in your church, in your community, and maybe even around the world. God calls all of us to heed God's vision. Don't lose that high vision. Let God's Spirit motivate and inspire you. Listen! Hear God's voice calling you today in new and challenging ways.

Pray that God will give each of us a mustard seed faith. We are blind to so much of life and we have not learned to see at all. We are often looking at life in such a negative way. Instead of being negative forces in society, or assuming that we cannot change or affect the evil forces

around us, let us see that God has called us to be the factor in our
world to challenge dogmatism, discrimination, racism, war, poverty, narrow religion, pollution, and corruption on all levels. Let us
follow the Christ-like way of love and service and never be satisfied
with canned religion or dogmatic statements about our faith. Let
us follow the vision of Christ who ever goes before us calling us to
higher places of service, new ways to love, and an awareness that
we will never "arrive" in our journey through life and in our quest
for meaning, but travel instead with an openness and expectancy
of new possibilities around every corner. Let us open our eyes to see
the possibilities within us, around us and before us. Most of all, may
we see the flaming power of God's Spirit leading us forward through
the difficult places of life. Let us open your eyes and ears. Listen and
see! Rise up and follow wherever God leads.

ALSO FROM ENERGION PUBLICATIONS
Guides to Practical Ministry

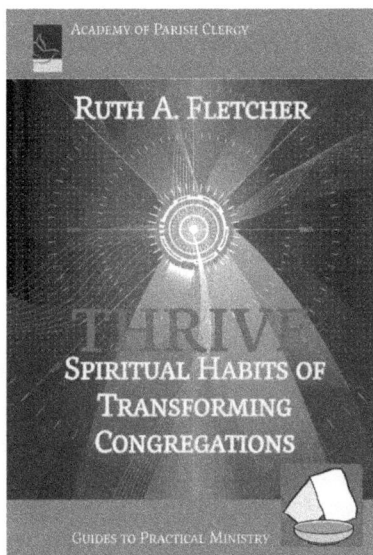

In this clear, concise and hope-filled book Ruth Fletcher offers substantive help and direction to congregational leaders and pastors alike. Grounded in her years of experience in a wide variety of church settings, her faithful observation of human life and her deep love of God, Ruth tells us stories of transformation that arise like green shoots from the most unexpected and unlikely of places.

Rev. Laurie Rudel
Pastor, Queen Anne
Christian Church
Seattle, Washington

FROM ANOTHER
ACADEMY OF PARISH CLERGY AUTHOR

Bob Cornwall provides a vision for today's Christians, centered around living out our gifts in creative and life-transforming ways. We are gifted, even when we are unaware of it.
Bruce Epperly, PhD
Pastor and Author

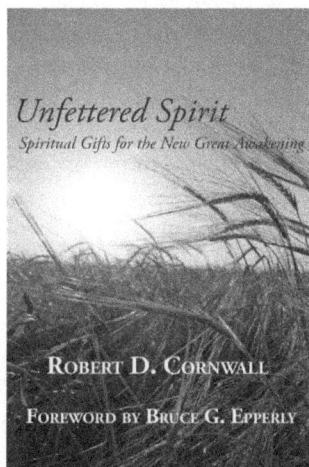

MORE FROM ENERGION PUBLICATIONS

ACADEMY OF PARISH CLERGY SERIES AND AUTHORS

Conversations in Ministry

Clergy Table Talk	Kent Ira Groff	$9.99
Out of the Office	Robert D. Cornwall	$9.99
Wind and Whirlwind	David Moffett-Moore	$9.99

Guides to Practical Ministry

Overcoming Sermon Block	William Powell Tuck	$12.99
Thrive	Ruth Fletcher	$14.99
In Changing Times	Ron Higdon	$14.99

Academy Member Authors (Selected Titles)

Faith in the Public Square	Robert D. Cornwall	$16.99
Ephesians: A Participatory Study Guide		$9.99
Ultimate Allegiance		$9.99
The Authority of Scripture in a Postmodern Age		$5.99
From Words of Woe to Unbelievable News		$5.99
The Eucharist		$5.99
Unfettered Spirit		$14.99
From Here to Eternity	Bruce Epperly	$5.99
Angels, Mysteries, and Miracles		$9.99
Transforming Acts		$14.99
Jonah: When God Changes		$5.99
Process Theology: Embracing Adventure with God		$5.99
The Journey to the Undiscovered Country	William Powell Tuck	$9.99
Lord, I Keep Getting a Busy Signal		$9.99
The Last Words from the Cross		$9.99
The Church Under the Cross		$9.99
Creation in Contemporary Experience	David Moffett-Moore	$9.99
Life as Pilgrimage		$14.99
The Spirit's Fruit		$9.99
The Jesus Manifesto		$9.99
Spiritual Care Reflections	Charles J. Lopez, Jr.	$14.99
Surviving a Son's Suicide	Ron Higdon	$9.99
All I Need to Know I'm Still Learning at 80		

Generous Quantity Discounts Available
Dealer Inquiries Welcome
Energion Publications — P.O. Box 841
Gonzalez, FL_ 32560
Website: http://energionpubs.com
Phone: (850) 525-3916

www.ingramcontent.com/pod-product-compliance
Lightning Source LLC
Chambersburg PA
CBHW022129080426
42734CB00006B/288